How to Extract Info, Secrets, and Truth:

Make People Reveal Their True Thoughts and Intentions Without Them Even Knowing It

By Patrick King
Social Interaction and Conversation Coach at
www.PatrickKingConsulting.com

Table of Contents

Chapter 1. Observe

Being a better communicator is one thing, but when you think about it, so much of what we "say" to one another is far beyond the verbal language we share intentionally. If you want to become better at reading people, and understand them on a deeper level, it's necessary to go one step deeper than what we normally think of as communication.

In the chapters that follow, we're going to explore several subtle but effective ways to quietly gather information about the people around us – even and especially when they're not deliberately sharing it! We'll look at the power of observation, how to master questioning techniques to your advantage, and see what we can learn from interrogators, interviewers and even cold readers and "psychics."

But first, we'll start with something simply: merely looking at what's right in front of you. If you *really look*, there's a lot of information to be gleaned about the people you interact with. The idea that people cannot help but reveal their true intentions and feelings one way or another is an appealing one. People can *say* whatever they like, but it's always been understood that "actions speak louder than words" and that people's facial expressions or body language can inadvertently reveal their deepest selves. We are in effect communicating all the time, sending out information about our intentions and feelings—but only a small fraction of this is verbal.

Observing people's actions and behavior in real time is what we most commonly understand to be analyzing people. It might seem natural to look to people's physical bodies in space to intuit what's going on in their heads, and there's plenty of scientific evidence to support these claims. Physical appearance can tell you a lot about a person's feelings, motivations, and fears, even if they're actively trying to conceal these. In other words, the body doesn't lie!

Nevertheless, this approach to understanding people's motivations is not foolproof. When we're interacting with others and trying to understand what makes them tick, it's important to be cautious in making assumptions. We're all individuals, and context is very important. Though we can use various methods to read facial expressions and body language, it pays to remember that no single piece of information is enough to "prove" anything, and that the art of reading people this way comes down to taking a holistic view of the full scenario as it unfolds in front of you.

Look at my Face

Let's begin with Haggard and Isaacs in the 1960s. They filmed couples' faces during therapy and noticed little expressions that could only be caught when the film was slowed down. Later on, Paul Ekman expandcd on his own theory on *microexpressions* and published a book, *Telling Lies.*

We all know how to read *macro*expressions—those facial movements that last up to four seconds in duration—but there are quicker, more fleeting expressions that are so fast, they could easily be missed by the untrained eye. According to Ekman, facial expressions are actually physiological reactions. These expressions occur even when you're not around anyone who could see them. He found that across cultures, people used microexpressions to display their emotions on their faces in very predictable ways—even when they were attempting to conceal them or even when they themselves were unaware of the emotion.

His research led him to believe that microexpressions are spontaneous, tiny contractions of certain muscle groups that are predictably related to emotions and are the same in all people, regardless of upbringing, background, or cultural expectation. They can be as quick as one-thirtieth of a second long. But catching them and understanding what they mean is a way to cut through what is merely said to get to the deeper truth of what people feel and believe. Macroexpressions can be, to some extent, forced or exaggerated, but microexpressions are understood to be more genuine and difficult to fake or else suggestive of concealed or rapidly changing emotions.

Within the brain, there are two neural pathways related to facial expressions.

The first is the *pyramidal tract*, responsible for voluntary expressions (i.e., most macroexpressions), and the *extrapyramidal tract*, responsible for involuntary emotional facial expressions (i.e., microexpressions). Researchers have discovered that individuals who experience intense emotional situations but also external pressure to control or hide that expression will show activity in *both* these brain pathways. This suggests that they're working against one another, with the more conscious and voluntary expressions dominating the involuntary ones. Nevertheless, some tiny expressions of the real emotion may "leak" out—this is what you're looking for when you attempt to read a person in this way.

So just exactly how does one learn to read these expressions? Can you really decode a person's deepest feelings just by looking at a twitch of their nose or a wrinkle in their brow?

According to Ekman, there are six universal human emotions, all with corresponding minuscule facial expressions. Happiness is seen in lifted cheeks, with the corners of the mouth raised up and back. Wrinkles appear under the eyes, between the upper lip and nose, and in the outside corner of the eyes. In other words, the movements we're all familiar with in an ordinary smile are there on a micro level too.

Microexpressions suggesting sadness are also what you'd expect. The outer corner of the eyes droops down, along with the corners of the lips. The lower lip may even tremble. Eyebrows may form a telltale triangle shape. For the emotion of disgust, the upper lip lifts and may be accompanied by wrinkles above it and wrinkles on the forehead. The eyes may narrow slightly as the cheeks are raised.

For anger, eyebrows lower and tense up, often at a downward angle. Eyes tighten, too, and the lips may be pursed or held stiffly open. The eyes are staring and piercing. Fear, on the other hand, entails similar contractions but upward. Whether open or closed, the mouth is tense, and both upper and lower eyelids are lifted. Finally, surprise or shock will show itself in elevated brows—rounded rather than triangular, like with sadness. The upper eyelids lift up and the lower eyelids stretch downward, opening the eyes wide. Sometimes, the jaw can hang loosely open.

As you can see, microexpressions are not very different from macroexpressions in the muscles that are involved; the main difference is in their speed. Ekman demonstrated, however, that these quick flashes of muscle contraction are so fast that people miss them: ninety-nine percent of people were unable to perceive them. Nevertheless, he also claims that people can be trained to look for microexpressions and in particular learn to detect liars, a classic example of saying one thing and feeling another.

Ekman claims to be able to teach his technique within thirty-two hours, but for those of us who are curious about using the principles in our own lives, it's easy to start. Firstly, look for discrepancies between what is said and what is actually demonstrated through facial expressions. For example, someone might be assuring you verbally and making promises but showing quick expressions of fear that betray their real position.

Other classic indicators that you are being lied to include lifting the shoulders slightly while someone is vehemently confirming the truth of what they're saying. Scratching the nose, moving the head to the side, avoiding eye contact, uncertainty in speaking, and general fidgeting also indicate someone's internal reality is not exactly lining up with the external—i.e., they might be lying.

Again, it's worth mentioning here that this is not a foolproof method and that research has mostly failed to find a strong relationship between body language, facial expression, and deceitfulness. No single gesture alone indicates anything. Many psychologists have since pointed out that discrepancies in microexpressions can actually indicate discomfort, nervousness, stress, or tension, without deception being involved.

Nevertheless, when used as a tool along with other tools, and when taken in context, microexpression analysis can be powerful. Granted, you'll need to stare quite intently at the person and observe them in a way that's uncomfortable and too obvious for normal social situations. You'll also have to weed out tons of irrelevant data and decide what gestures count as "noise" or meaningless idiosyncrasies.

At any rate, people who lack the required training have been shown to be astoundingly bad at spotting liars—despite feeling as though their gut intuitions about others' deceit is reliable. This means that even a slight increase in accuracy you might gain from understanding and implementing the microexpression theory may make all the difference. A microexpression may be small, but it's still a data point.

All this talk of unmasking liars may make this technique seem rather combative and underhanded, but Ekman is careful to point out that "lies" and "deceit," as he frames them, can also indicate the hiding of an emotion and not necessarily any malicious intent. There is certainly an allure in playing detective and uncovering people's secret feelings, but in reality, the use of microexpression analysis is a bit like CSI: it always looks a bit more impressive on TV than it is in real life.

Furthermore, the goal in developing the skill of microexpression analysis is not to play "gotcha!" to our friends and colleagues, but rather to enhance our own empathy and emotional intelligence and foster a richer understanding of the people around us.

If you're not convinced about using microexpressions to detect deception, another perspective is not to look for lies or classify expressions according to their duration, but rather to look at what an expression typically conveys. Then, depending on context and how the expression compares to what's said *verbally*, you can come to your own conclusions.

Nervousness is typically behind things like tightening the lips or twitching the corners of the mouth very quickly toward the ear and back. Quivering lips or chin, a furrowed brow, narrowed eyes, and pulled-in lips may also indicate the person is feeling tense. If a person you know is normally calm and composed but you suddenly notice plenty of these little signs while they tell you a tale you don't quite believe, you might infer that, for some reason, they're nervous about telling it to you. Whether this is because they're lying or because their story is simply uncomfortable to tell—only you can decide from context.

A person feeling dislike or disagreement might purse their lips tightly, roll their eyes, flutter their eyelids briefly, or crinkle their nose. They may also squint a little or narrow their eyes like a cartoon villain staring down the hero, close their eyes, or "sneer" a little in a slight expression of disdain. If a person opens the Christmas present you gave them and immediately proceeds to do all of the above, you might want to assume they don't really like their gift, despite what they say to the contrary.

Those dealing with stress may find tiny ways to release that stress, giving themselves away even though for the most part they appear quite calm. Uncontrollable, fast blinking and making repetitive motions like twitching the cheek, biting the tongue, or touching parts of the face with their fingers can all indicate someone who's finding a particular situation stressful. This might make sense when someone's in a job interview or being questioned in connection with a crime but may be more noteworthy if you spot it in seemingly calm situations. This discrepancy gives you a clue that all might not be as it appears.

Pay attention also to asymmetry in facial expressions. Natural, spontaneous, and genuine expressions of emotion tend to be symmetrical. Forced, fake, or conflicting expressions tend not to be. And again, try to interpret what you see in context, and consider the whole person, including other body language.
Remember that analyzing facial expressions is a powerful method of understanding

others that's more than "skin-deep," but it's not foolproof. Every observation you make is simply a data point and doesn't prove anything either way. The skill comes in gathering as much data as you can and interpreting the whole, emerging pattern before you, rather than just one or two signs. For this reason, it's best to use what you know about microexpressions as a supplement to other methods and tools.

Body Talk

Body language, for instance, may be just as powerful a language to learn to read and comprehend as facial expressions. After all, the face is simply a part of the body. Why focus on just one part when people's postures and general movements can speak just as eloquently? Ex-FBI agent Joe Navarro is generally considered an authority in this field and has used his experience to teach others about the wealth of information people share without ever opening their mouths (i.e., what he calls "nonverbal communication").

Originally from Cuba and having to learn English after moving to the U.S. when he was eight years old, Navarro quickly came to appreciate how the human body was "a kind of billboard that advertised what a person was thinking." During his career he spoke at length about learning to spot people's "tells"—those little movements that suggest that someone is uncomfortable, hostile, relaxed, or fearful.

As with facial expressions, these tells may hint at deceit or lies but primarily indicate that someone is uncomfortable or that there is a discrepancy between what's felt and what's expressed. Armed with an understanding of how body language works, we can not only open up new channels on which to communicate with others, but pay attention to our own bodies and the messages we may be unwittingly sending to others.

Firstly, it's important to understand that nonverbal communication is inbuilt, biological, and the result of evolution. Our emotional responses to certain things are lightning-fast, and they happen spontaneously, whether we want them to or not. Importantly, they express themselves physically in the way we hold and move our bodies in space, potentially resulting in the transmission of thousands of nonverbal messages.

It's the more primitive, emotional, and perhaps honest part of our brain, the limbic brain, that's responsible for these automatic responses. While the prefrontal cortex (the more intellectual and abstract part) is a little removed from the body, and more under conscious control, it's also the part that's capable of lying. But even though a person can say one thing, their bodies will always speak the truth. If you can tune into the gestures, movements, postures, patterns of touching, and even the clothing a person wears, you give yourself a more direct channel into what they *really* think and feel. Navarro claims that the majority of communication is nonverbal anyway— meaning you're actively missing out on the bulk of the message by *not* considering body language.

Consider that communication started out nonverbally. In our earliest histories, before the development of language, humankind most likely communicated by gestures, simple sounds, and facial expressions. In fact, from the moment a baby is born it instinctively makes faces to communicate that it's cold, hungry, or frightened. We never need to be taught how to read basic gestures or understand tones of voice—this is because nonverbal communication was our first communication and may still be our preferred form.

Think of all the ways you already take nonverbal communication for granted—in the way you show love or demonstrate your anger. Even if you aren't aware of it, we are all still processing vast amounts of information on nonverbal channels. Learn how to read this information and you can determine if someone is trying to deceive you or perhaps if someone is trying to conceal their feelings and true intentions from you.

You've probably heard of the "fight-or-flight" response before, but there's a third possibility: freeze. What's more, these responses to danger may be quite subtle, but nevertheless, they speak to discomfort and fear. Our ancestors might have shown fight-or-flight when running from predators or enemy tribes, but those instincts might have followed us into the boardroom or classroom.

The limbic brain is again responsible for these fear responses. Someone who is asked a difficult question or put on the spot may look like a deer caught in headlights. They may lock their legs around a chair and stay fixed tight in that position (this is the freeze response). Another possibility is physically moving the body away from what is perceived as threatening. A person may put an object on their lap or position their limbs toward the exit (the flight response). Finally, a third person may "fight." This aggressive response to fear can show itself in picking arguments, verbally "sparring," or adopting threatening gestures.

In fact, the more competent you become at reading nonverbal signals, the more you may come to appreciate how fundamentally *physical* they are and how much they speak to our shared evolutionary history. In the past we might have literally fended off an attack with certain gestures or indeed set out to attack another with very obvious movements and expressions. These days, our world is very abstract and the things that threaten us are more verbal and conceptual—but the old machinery for expression, fear, aggression, curiosity, etc. is all still there, only perhaps expressed a little more subtly.

Let's consider what are called "pacifying behaviors." These can offer a key insight into someone who is feeling stressed, unsure, or threatened. Essentially, a pacifying behavior is what it sounds like—the (unconscious) attempt to self-soothe in the face of some perceived threat. When we feel stressed, our limbic brain may compel us to make little gestures designed to calm us: touching the forehead, rubbing the neck, fiddling with hair, or wringing the hands are all behaviors intended to soothe stress.

The neck is a vulnerable area of the body, but one that is relatively exposed. Consider how aggressive people "go for the jugular" and you understand how the throat and neck can be unconsciously felt to be an area open for fatal attack. It makes sense then that someone unconsciously covering or stroking this area is expressing their struggle, emotional discomfort, or insecurity. Men may use this gesture more often than women; men may fidget with their ties or squeeze the top of the neck, while women may put the fingers to the suprasternal notch (the indent between the collarbones) or play nervously with a necklace.

Pay attention to this behavior and you'll notice how it reveals someone's fears and insecurities in real-time. Someone might say something a little aggressive and another person responds by leaning back slightly, crossing the arms, and putting one hand up to the throat. Notice this in real-time and you can infer that this particular statement has aroused some fear and uncertainty.

Similarly, rubbing or touching the forehead or temples can signal emotional distress or overwhelm. A quick tap with the fingers may reveal a momentary feeling of stress, whereas a prolonged cradling of the head in both hands can spell extreme distress. In fact, you can consider any cradling, stroking, or rubbing movement as the physical clue of a person's need to self-pacify. This could mean touching cheeks when the person feels nervous or frightened, rubbing or licking the lips, massaging the earlobes, or running the fingers through the hair or beard.

Pacifying behaviors are not just things liked stroking or rubbing, though. Puffing out the cheeks and exhaling loudly is also a gesture that releases considerable stress. Have you ever noticed how many people will do this after hearing bad news or narrowly escaping an accident? An unexpected stress release response is yawning—rather than indicating boredom, the body's sudden attempt to draw in more oxygen during stressful times is even seen in other animals. "Leg cleansing" is another, and it entails wiping down the legs as though to wash them or brush off dust. This can be missed if it's hidden under a table, but if you can notice it, it is a strong indication of an attempt to self-soothe during stressful moments.

"Ventilating" is another behavior you may not pay much attention to. Notice someone pulling their shirt collar away from their neck or tossing the hair away from the shoulders as though to cool off. They're likely experiencing discomfort or tension.

Though this might be literally because of an uncomfortable environment, it's more likely a response to inner tension and stress that needs "cooling off."

One of the most obvious forms of pacifying behavior looks exactly like what a mother might do to a young child to soothe them: cradling and hugging one's own body or rubbing the shoulders as though to ward off a chill all suggest a person who feels under threat, worried, or overwhelmed—these gestures are an unconscious way to protect the body.

This is an important underlying principle across all of body language theory: that limbs and gestures may signal unconscious attempts to protect and defend the body. When you consider that the torso contains all the body's vital organs, you can understand why the limbic brain has reflex responses to shield this area when threats are perceived—even emotional threats.

Someone who is highly unresponsive to a request or who feels attacked or criticized may cross their arms as if to say, "Back off." Raising the arms to the chest during an argument is a classic blocking gesture, almost as if the words being exchanged were literally thrown, causing an unconscious reflex to fend them off. On a similar note, slumping, loose arms can indicate defeat, disappointment, or despair. It's as though the body is physically broadcasting the nonphysical sentiment of "I can't do this. I don't know what to do. I give up."

Let's take it further. Imagine someone standing over a desk, arms spread wide. Aren't you immediately reminded of an animal claiming territory? Wide, expansive gestures signal confidence, assertiveness, and even dominance. If a person is standing with arms akimbo, they leave their torso exposed. This is a powerful way to communicate that they are confident in taking up room and don't feel threatened or unsure in the least.

Other gestures of confidence and assertiveness include that favorite of politicians and businessmen the world over: "hand steepling." The fingertips are pressed together so they form a little steeple. It's the classic negotiating gesture, signaling confidence, poise, and certainty about your power and position, as though the hands were merely resting and calmly contemplating their next move.

On the other hand (pun intended) wringing and rubbing the hands is more likely to demonstrate a lack of feeling in control or doubt in one's own abilities. Again, this is a pacifying gesture designed to release tension. Hands are our tools to effect change in the world and bring about our actions. When we fidget, wring our hands, or clench our fists, we are demonstrating a lack of ease and confidence in our abilities or find it difficult to act confidently.

What about the legs? These are often overlooked since they might be concealed under a desk, but legs and feet are powerful indicators too. "Happy feet" can bounce and jiggle—on the other hand, bouncy legs paired with other nervous or pacifying gestures may indicate an excess of nervous tension and energy or impatience . . . or too much coffee, you decide. Toes that point upward can be thought of as "smiling" feet and indicate positive, optimistic feelings.

Physiologically, our legs and feet are all about, unsurprisingly, movement. Busy feet could suggest an unexpressed desired to get moving, either literally or figuratively! It's also been said that feet point in the direction they unconsciously wish to go. Both toes turned toward the conversation partner can signal "I'm here with you; I'm present in this conversation" whereas feet angled toward an exit could be a clue that the person really would prefer to leave.

Other clues that someone is wanting to move, leave, or escape are gestures like clasping the knees, rocking up and down on the balls of the feet, or standing with a bit of a bounce in the step—all of these subtly communicate someone whose unconscious mind has "fired up the engines" and wants to get going. This could mean they're excited about possibilities and want to get started as soon as possible, or they may have a strong dislike for the current situation and almost literally want to "run away." Again, context matters!

Legs and feet can also reveal negative emotions. Crossing the legs, as with the arms, can signal a desire to close off or protect the body from a perceived threat or discomfort. Crossed legs are often tilted toward a person we like and trust—and away from someone we don't. This is because the legs can be used as a barrier, either warding off or welcoming in someone's presence. Women may dangle shoes off the tips of the toes in flirtatious moments, slipping a shoe on and off the heel again. Without getting too Freudian about it, the display of feet and legs can indicate comfort and even intimacy with someone. On the other hand, locking the feet and ankles can be part of a freeze response when someone *really* doesn't like a situation or person.

So having discussed the face, hands, legs and feet, and torso in general, what else is there? Turns out, a lot more. The body as a whole can be positioned in space in certain ways, held in certain postures, or brought further or closer to other people. The next time you meet someone new, lean in to shake their hand and then watch what they do with their entire body.

If they "stand their ground" and stay where they are, they're demonstrating comfort with the situation, you, and themselves. Taking a step back or turning the entire torso and feet to the side suggests that you may have gotten too close for their comfort. They may even take a step closer, signaling that they are happy with the contact and may even escalate it further.

The general principle is pretty obvious: bodies expand when they are comfortable, happy, or dominant. They contract when unhappy, fearful, or threatened. Bodies move toward what they like and away from what they don't like. Leaning toward a person can show agreement, comfort, flirtation, ease, and interest. Likewise, crossing the arms, turning away, leaning back, and using tightly crossed legs as a barrier show a person's unconscious attempt to get away from or protect themselves from something unwanted. Those people who spread out on public transport? They feel relaxed, secure, and confident (annoying, isn't it?).

Those that seem to bundle themselves as tightly as possible may instead signal low confidence and assertiveness, as though they were always trying to take up less room. Similarly puffing up the chest and holding out the arms in an aggressive posture communicates, "Look how big I am!" in an argument, whereas raising the shoulders and "turtling" in on oneself is nonverbally saying, "Please don't hurt me! Look how small I am!"

We're not much like gorillas in the forest, beating our chests during heated arguments—but if you look closely, you may still see faint clues to this more primal behavior anyway. Those postures that take up room and expand are all associated with dominance, assertiveness, and authority. Hands on the hips, hands held regally behind the back (doesn't it make you think of royalty or a dignified soldier who is unafraid of attack?), or even arms laced behind the neck as one leans back in a chair—all signify comfort and dominance.

When you are becoming aware of people's body language, ask in the first instance whether their actions, gestures, and postures are constricting or expanding. Is the face open or closed? Are the hands and arms spread wide and held loose and far from the body, or are the limbs kept close and tense? Is the facial expression you're looking at pulled tight or loose and open? Is the chin held high (sign of confidence) or tucked in (sign of uncertainty)?

Imagine you have no words at all to describe what you're looking at; just observe. Is the body in front of you relaxed and comfortable in space, or is there some tightness, tension, and unease in the way the limbs are held?
A lot of the art of body language is, once pointed out, rather intuitive. This is because each of us is actually already fluent in its interpretation. It is merely allowing ourselves to de-emphasize the verbal for a moment to take notice of the wealth of nonverbal information that's always flowing between people. None of it is really concealed. Rather, it's a question of opening up to data coming in on a channel we are not taught to pay attention to.

Putting it All Together

How can we use all of this to actually help us "read" people effectively and understand even those motivations, intentions, and feelings people may be actively trying to conceal? It's worth remembering right off the bat that detecting deception is not as straightforward as some would have you believe and, as we've seen, not as simple as spotting a tell-tale sign that proves a lie once and for all. Laypeople and professionals alike are notoriously bad at reading body language, despite the wealth of information we now have on the topic.

But the knack really comes in deciding what to do with certain observations once you've made them. Does a person's folded arms mean they're lying, unhappy about something, fearful . . . or just feeling cold? The trick comes in using not just one or two but a whole host of clues and tells to form a more comprehensive picture of behavior. The reason why it's so difficult to "spot a lie" with perfect accuracy is that the gestures and expressions associated with deception are often not different from those signifying stress or discomfort.
So given all this, is it worth learning to read body language? Absolutely.

Adding this extra dimension to your interactions with others will only enrich your relationships and give you extra insight into your interpersonal conflicts and tensions. Knowing what's going on with another person allows you to be a better communicator and speak to what people are actually feeling rather than what they're merely saying.

Body language signals are always there. Every person is communicating nonverbally, at every moment of the day. And it is possible to not only observe this information in real-time but learn to properly synthesize and interpret it. You don't need to be an expert, and you don't need to be perfect. You just need to pay attention and be curious about your fellow human beings in a way you might not have before. As you're developing your body language reading skills, it may help to keep a few key principles in mind:

Establish normal behavior.

One or two gestures in a conversation don't mean much. They could be accidental or purely physiological. But the more you know how someone "normally" behaves, the more you can assume that any behavior outside of this is worth looking more closely at. If someone *always* squints their eyes, pouts, jiggles their feet, or clears their throat, you can more or less discount these gestures.

Look for unusual or incongruent behavior.

Reading people is about reading patterns of behavior. Pay special attention to clues that are unusual for that person. Suddenly fiddling with the hair and avoiding eye contact could tell you something is going on, especially if this person never does either of these things normally. You may with time come to recognize "tells" in people closest to you—they may always wrinkle their nose when being dishonest or clear their throat excessively when they're afraid and pretending not to be.

Importantly, pay close attention to those gestures and movements that seem incongruous. Discrepancies between verbal and nonverbal communication can tell you more than merely observing nonverbal communication alone. It's about context. An obvious example is someone wringing their hands, rubbing their temples, and sighing loudly but who claims, "I'm fine. Nothing's wrong." It's not the gestures that tell you this person is concealing distress, but the fact that they're incongruent with the words spoken.

Gather plenty of data.

As we've seen, certain constricting behaviors could merely be because one is cold, tired, or even ill, and expansive gestures may not be about confidence so much as feeling physically warm and wanting to cool off. This is why it's important to never interpret a gesture alone. Always consider clusters of clues. If you see something, note it but don't come to any conclusions immediately. Look to see if they do it again. Look for other gestures that may reinforce what you've seen or else give evidence for the opposite interpretation. Check to see if the behavior repeats itself with other people or in other contexts. Take your time to really *analyze* the whole of what's in front of you.

Look for mirroring.

An important thing to remember is that certain gestures may mean one thing in one context or when shown to one person but have a different meaning in another context or with someone else. In other words, certain gestures could literally only apply to you as you speak to this person. If you're not very familiar with someone, a quick body language–reading shortcut is to merely notice whether they are or are not mirroring your gestures, whatever they are.

Mirroring is a fundamental human instinct; we tend to match and mimic the behavior and expressions of those we like or agree with, while we don't if we dislike a person or perceive them negatively. If you're in a meeting with a new client, you may notice that no matter how friendly your voice or how often you smile and make open-handed, warm gestures, they respond with coldness and closed gestures, failing to mirror back to you your optimism. Here, the gestures themselves are irrelevant; it's the fact that they are not shared which shows you that the person you're dealing with is unreceptive, hostile, or threatened.

Pay attention to energy.

This is not some fluffy, esoteric idea; in a group, simply take note of where intention, effort, and focus are being concentrated.

Watch where energy flows. Sometimes, the "leader" of a group is only so in name; the real power may lie elsewhere. One only needs to look at how much focus and attention flows toward a baby in the room to see this in action—the baby says and does very little yet nevertheless commands the attention of everyone there.

Similarly, a family may have the father as the official "leader," and he may gesture and talk loudly to cement this perception. But pay attention and you may see that it's his wife who is constantly deferred to, and every member of the family may show with their body language that it is in fact their mother's needs that take precedence, despite what's claimed verbally.
The most powerful voice in a room is not necessarily the loudest. A lot can be understood about the power dynamics in a group by watching to see where energy flows. Who speaks the most? Who are people always speaking *to*, and how? Who always seems to take "center stage"?

Remember that body language is dynamic.

When we speak, the content of our language isn't just about the words and the grammar we use to string them together. It's about *how* we talk. Do we say a lot or a little? What tone of voice? Are sentences long and complicated or short and terse? Is everything phrased tentatively, like a question, or is it stated confidently, as though it's a known fact? What's the speed of delivery? How loud? Is it clear or mumbling?

In the same way that verbal information can vary in the way it's communicated, nonverbal information can vary too. Gestures are not static, fixed things but living expressions that move in time and space. Watch the flow of information in real-time. Watch how expressions change and move in response to the environment and those in it. Don't be curious about "catching" a discreet gesture, but rather watch the flow of gestures as they change.

For example, look at how a person walks. Walking is like a body posture but set in motion. Shuffling, slow gaits suggest lack of confidence, while springy, quick ones suggest optimism and excitement. Become interested in how a person responds to others in conversation or their style of talking to those in positions of power. Once you start looking, you'll be amazed at the wealth of information that's just waiting there to be noticed.

Context is everything.

Finally, it bears repeating: no gesture occurs in a vacuum. Nonverbal communication needs to be considered in relation to everything else—just like verbal communication. Establish patterns and learn about a person's behavior over time, in different contexts, and toward different people. Consider the situation and environment—sweating and stuttering during your wedding vows or a big interview is understandable; doing so when asked to explain what you're doing snooping through someone's drawers is a little more suspicious.

Remember that everyone has their own unique, idiosyncratic personality. Factor into your analysis the fact that people are either introverted or extroverted, may favor emotions or intellect, may have high or low tolerance for risk and adversity, may thrive in stressful situations or wither in them, and may be spontaneous and casual or goal-directed and rather serious. Our instinctual, evolutionarily programmed impulses can't be hidden or resisted, but they can take on slightly different forms depending on our unique personalities.

Admittedly, reading facial expressions and body language is a skill that takes time and patience to master. There are no quick and easy tricks to understanding people's deeper motivations. However, remember the above principles and focus on honing your powers of observation, and you'll soon develop a knack for seeing and understanding even tiny ripples and flutters of behavior you might have previously missed. We live in a world dominated by words and language. But when you become a student of nonverbal communication, it's no exaggeration to say that you open yourself up to an entirely different, sometimes quite strange world.

The Human Body is a Whole—Read It that Way

Everyone has heard an offhand statistic which sounds a little something like, "Ninety percent of your communication is really nonverbal." We imagine that communication is primarily a question of language, symbols, noises and sounds, and images on a page, whereas the person creating the language is a separate physical entity occupying space.

But in reality, the boundary between verbal and non-verbal, medium and message, is always a little blurred.
In the previous sections, we've explicitly considered how a person can be "read" even beyond the content they are choosing to deliberately convey to you. In other words, you're not just listening to the message they're sending, but listening to *them*, as though their body itself were something to read and interpret.

In the discussion on detecting deceit or hidden true feelings, we made an assumption: that what is inside a person will invariably manifest itself somehow on the outside of a person. This is because we instinctively understand that human beings are *wholes*, i.e., the verbal and nonverbal are really just different aspects of the same thing. What really is the distinction between the words and the lips that say them? The body and the gesture that the body makes?

This may seem a little abstract, but it turns out there's now interesting research to back up the idea that communication as a whole can be understood as a complete expression of a human being. First of all, have you ever had a phone call with someone where you could instantly tell whether they were smiling or not? Call center managers will tell their staff that people can "hear smiles" over the phone, but how do you suppose this is actually possible?

It makes sense when we consider that a voice is not an abstract symbol, but a real, physiological part of the human body. Researcher at the Donders Institute of Radboud University Wim Pouw published some interesting findings in the *PNAS* journal in 2020. He was interested in the topic we all seem to instinctively understand: that hand gestures and facial expressions can help us better understand what is being communicated—in fact at times a gesture can be fundamental to us understanding the message.

In an experiment, Pouw asked six people to make a simple noise (like "aaaaa") but to pair it with different arm and hand gestures as they spoke. He then asked thirty other participants to listen to recordings of the sounds only. Surprisingly, the participants were able to guess what the accompanying movements were and even mimic them for themselves. They could say what the movement was, where it was performed and even how quickly the gesture was made!

How? Pouw's theory is that people are able to unconsciously detect subtle but important shifts in voice pitch and volume, as well as speed changes, that accompany different gestures. When you make a gesture, your *whole body* gets involved, including your voice. In other words, when you hear a voice, you are hearing multiple aspects about that person's body.

When speaking, sound vibrates all through the connective tissues of your body, but differences in muscle tension can arise if we are making gestures with other parts of our body, and we can hear these tiny adjustments in the voice. The great thing about this particular skill is that you don't necessarily need to train it, just become aware of it. You probably never thought you could practice reading body language over the phone, but you can—if you understand that the voice is simply a part of a person's body!

Voice alone is an incredibly rich aspect of behavior to study. When you hear someone from another room, on a recording or over the phone, close your eyes and imagine what their body is doing, and what that posture or gesture might indicate. You can undoubtedly hear age and sex through voice, too, but you can also infer something about a person's ethnicity or nationality by listening to their accent or vocabulary.

Listen to the speed, timbre, volume, pitch and degree of control used. How is the person breathing? How are their words and the *way* they're saying those words reinforcing one another, or perhaps undermining one another? For example someone on the phone might be telling you how excited they are about something, but their slow and sluggish voice may suggest to you that they're slouching and folded in on themselves—and greatly overstating their excitement.

Thinking in Terms of Message Clusters

Let's shift our attention away from individual physical actions that may or not mean or suggest something else, and instead consider human behavior in terms of the overall message it communicates to others. If we are feeling hostile and aggressive, for example, this attitude and intention will show up in every area, from our language to our actions to our facial expressions to our voice. Rather than trying to imagine what every possible manifestation of aggression looks like, we can focus on the aggression itself, and watch for resulting clusters of behavior.

Aggression is understandably shown by confronting gestures, or those that move actively and energetically *towards* a target. Invasive, approaching gestures that move in on another person can signify an attempt to dominate, control or attack. Verbally, this could look like an insult or a jeer, physically it looks like standing too close, or even displaying or exposing oneself as if to demonstrate superior strength. Aggression is all about sudden, impactful and targeted gestures. It's as though the entire body is clenched around a single pointed intention.

Assertive body language, on the other hand, is as forceful but not so directed. This is a person standing their ground, i.e., being firm, balanced, smooth and open in expression of a confidently held desire. The aggressive person may yell, whereas an assertive one may simply state their business with a kind of muscular certainty that can be heard in the voice.

Submissive body language is the complement—look for "lowering," self-protective gestures that make the person seems smaller, with small, appeasing gestures like smiling excessively, being motionless, speaking quietly, turning the eyes downward or assuming a vulnerable or non-threatening stance.

This is different from being genuinely **open and receptive**. Relaxed, friendly people will signal looseness—open and uncrossed arms and legs, unguarded facial expressions, easy speech, or even loosening or removing outer layers of clothing to show informality.

This is a little like **romantic** body language, except someone who is sexually interested will also behave in ways that emphasize intimacy. The focus will be on sensuality (touching the other person or the self, preening, stroking, slowing down, warm smiles) and connection (prolonged eye contact, questions, agreement, mirroring). The overwhelming perception is that of an invitation to close distance.

Deceptive body language is anything that is characterized by a sense of tension. Deceit is the existence of two conflicting things— for example someone believes one thing but says another. Look for the tension that such a disparity creates. You want to look for anxiety, closed body language, and a sense of distractedness (after all, they are processing extra data they don't want to reveal to you!). Look for someone who appears to be trying hard to control themselves, with an anxious effect.

By looking at intentions behind overall communication, we can start to read the body as a whole. This makes it easier to gather multiple data points more quickly, and find patterns of behavior rather than inferring too much from just a single gesture or expression. Consider the entire human body—the limbs, the face, the voice, the posture, the torso, the clothing, the hair, the hands and fingers, everything.

Can you see a cluster of closed off, defensive gestures? Is someone trying to display power, strength and dominance? Or are they just confident? Is the person in front of you trying to show that they are trustworthy, or that they have a truly valuable thing to sell you (salesman's body language) or that they are greeting you with openness and respect?

In very general terms, look for the following *whole body* patterns:

- Crossing, closing in, or shutting off – could signal guardedness, suspicion, shyness

- Expanding, opening, loosening – signals friendliness, comfort, trust, relaxation
- Forward, pointed, directed – may speak to dominance, control, persuasiveness
- Preening, touching, stroking – shows romantic intentions
- Striking, abruptness, force, loudness – signal energy or violence, sometimes fear
- Repeating, agreement, mirroring – shows respect, friendliness, admiration, submission

In an even broader sense, look at overall behavior and communication as an expression of holding—holding on to, holding in, holding up, holding back, failing to hold, holding tightly, etc. If you meet someone whose entire being seems to be an expression of force and control (holding onto), you can take your interpretation of them from here, and better understand all the smaller data points—the hand wringing, the tightened and pursed lips, the furrowed brow, the shallow breathing that seems to strangle the voice, the high pitched tone, the rapid blinking . . .

Their body is sending you one clear, uniform message: one of tension. There's something big going on that they're trying hard to keep under wraps. Further context clues could tell you whether this is an uncomfortable admission, a lie, or simply something they're embarrassed about sharing with you.

Wrapping up, how can we read and analyze people just through sight and observation? We have covered two primary aspects: facial expressions and body language. It's important to note that though many aspects have been scientifically proven (with physiological origins), we can't say that simple observations are foolproof. It can never be definitive because there are too many external factors to take into account. But we can better understand what typical things to look for and what we can glean from them.

We use two types of facial expressions: micro- and macroexpressions. Macroexpressions are larger, slower, and more obvious. They are also routinely faked and consciously created. Microexpressions are the opposite of all of those things: incredibly quick, almost unperceivable, and unconscious. Psychologist Paul Ekman identified a host of microexpressions for each of the six basic emotions and in particular has also identified microexpressions to indicate nervousness, lying, or deception.

Body language has a much broader range of possible interpretations. Generally, a relaxed body takes up space, while an anxious body contracts and wants to conceal and comfort itself. There are too many specifics to list individually, but just keep in mind that the only true way to analyze body language is to first know exactly what someone is like when they are normal – and then compare back to that baseline.

To put everything together, we need to read the body *as a whole*, and look for general clusters of behavior that work together to communicate a unified message. The voice can be read like other body language. Look for signs or cues that are incongruent and don't mesh well with the other cues they're giving, this might reveal that the other person is trying to hide something if you can notice other cues that reaffirm this conclusion. However, as always, the signs you've picked up on could well be meaningless, so make sure you have enough data to support them.

People who have mastered the art of observation are like detectives, simultaneously gathering as much data as possible that they then constantly sift through, looking for broad, overall patterns that explain the whole picture in front of them. People are complex and constantly shifting and responding to their environment. But if you take the time to pay attention to how they engage with that environment – in *all* ways – you may surprise yourself with what you can learn. In the next chapter, we'll be looking at ways to not just observe behavior, but to actively influence it using the power of targeted questions.

Takeaways

- It's possible to extract loads of useful information from people merely by using the power of observation.
- First, observe the face, tiny, quick and involuntary movements of the face can "leak" a person's true emotions – there are six universal ones: anger, fear, surprise, disgust, happiness. Look for microexpressions that contradict what is said verbally.
- Ex-FBI agent Joe Navarro has some tips for reading body language, and they come from an understanding that body language is inbuilt, automatic and ancient, and based on fight, flight or freeze response in humans. For examples, "pacifying behaviors" like
- covering the neck can indicate the person is trying to manage stress.
- Note how the body is occupying space, and whether it is generally closed or open. Posture and gesture can tell you about whether a person is assertive, aggressive, uncertain or fearful. Bodies expand when they are comfortable, happy, or dominant. They contract when unhappy, fearful, or threatened.

- Body language signals cannot be interpreted in isolation. Rather, first seek a baseline of behavior to help interpret a particular new observation – a baseline helps you identify incongruent behavior and spot a deception.
- Look for mirroring, pay attention to overall energy, and remember that body language is dynamic, so you need to gather as much data as possible. Then consider this data in context of history and the current environment.
- The voice is a part of the human body and speed, timbre, volume, pitch, and degree of control can signify emotional state. The body is a whole, with verbal and nonverbal mingling together.
- Reading "message clusters" helps us organize isolated observations, and note whether they are aggressive, romantic, assertive, deceptive ad so on, in aggregate.

Chapter 2. Ask

Observations allow you to gather the "low hanging fruit" when it comes to information about people. A lot of what you want to know is right there for the seeing. Questions, however, take things a step further and actively elicit information from people, note merely observing their reaction to their environment but creating a stimulus that they respond to. The great thing about questions is that you can *target and guide* the person in front of you, so they share with you a response you can analyze more closely.

The most skillful form of questioning, as you can probably guess, is subtle and natural so it is never detected. Ordinary conversation can conceal your more deliberate intentions, if only you ask questions that seem relaxed, unobtrusive and appropriate to the situation. In the same way that we can miss valuable information about others because we simply don't observe what's right in front of us, we can also fail to understand those around because we're not really *listening* when they respond to us.

Through innocent questioning, we can uncover a host of information that represents an entire worldview or set of values. For instance, what if you were to ask someone where they obtained their news and which television channel, which set of publications, which magazines, and which pundits or hosts they preferred? It's a prime illustration of an indirect question that lets you understand quite a bit about how they think.

Yes, it involves a bit of extrapolation and guesswork, but at least there's a concrete piece of information to go on and many concrete associations with it. The answer to one question spurs another, more targeted question, and so on. Combined with the observation techniques already covered, you can see how a simple interaction can provide a rich, three dimensional view of a person.

We start this chapter with some of these indirect questions before going even more in-depth by asking people for stories and seeing what we can glean from those. These questions are phrased to challenge and inspire deep thought. They ask people to dive deeper so that we can begin to understand their behavioral and thought patterns.

1. What kind of prize would you work hardest for, and what punishment would you work hardest to avoid?

The answer to this question might help identify the true motive behind an individual's drive. Beyond surface-level things, what is really motivating people? What do they really care about? And what type of pain or pleasure matters to them? On an instinctual level, what really matters the most in both a positive and negative way? In a way, this answer also reflects values.

For example, gamblers all want one prize: the jackpot. They try and try again, whether it be with scratchers or slot machines to try and win the big prize money. Are they motivated by winning back their losses? Is their hope to become richer than they can imagine? Do they actually want it, or are they filling a void and keeping themselves distracted?

Why are they working so hard? You might surmise that their motivation is the thrill and rush of the risk involved. Do they care about making steady pay or finding their purpose? Maybe, and maybe not. When you can dig into what someone wants the most and why, you can often find what is driving them without having to ask it directly. The way people answer this question will clearly tell you their priorities and what they consider pain and pleasure in their lives.

Look for the emotion behind people's answers here, and you can get a pretty good read on their values. A goal of rising to CEO-level doesn't just exist in a vacuum—what are the feelings, emotions, and fulfilled expectations that come from wanting it? Likewise, wanting to avoid being poor speaks to very specific desires for security and safety from danger.

2. Where do you want to spend money, and where do you accept skimping on or skipping altogether?

This answer reveals what matters to someone's life and what they want to experience or avoid. This is not really about the item or items to be purchased; there comes a point where material belongings no longer have a use, and it's about what those items represent and provide. For example, sometimes, spending money on experiences instead of a new purse has the potential to improve someone's overall well-being and outlook on life. Again, look for the underlying emotions and motivations behind the answer.

So what do you have no problem splurging on, and what doesn't matter to you? For instance, when deciding on vacation expenditures, people may opt to splurge on an epic boat excursion and stay in a shabby hotel. This reveals their desire to experience an unforgettable moment rather than staying in a nice hotel with golden toilets, which they view as a waste of money. Others might opt for the opposite and revel in their creature comforts while not seeing much of the scenery. In either case, they've used their money to quite literally identify and spend toward their priorities and values.

Where your money goes is an important part of what makes you happy, so if you can pay attention to where you let it flow and where you cut it off, you'll immediately know what matters to you on a daily basis. Contrast this question to if you were to ask someone, "What do you value in your daily life?" Again, there is a concrete answer here to analyze.

This same principle applies equally to time, money, and effort. Where these things flow, whether consciously or unconsciously, represents the values people possess.

3. What is your most personally significant and meaningful achievement and also your most meaningful disappointment or failure?

It's common that experiences, whether they're good or bad, shape people into who they are. Achievements and failures tie into how someone sees oneself. Significant experiences also tend to create their self-identities—*you are this kind of person because you did this and succeeded or failed.* We can't escape the fact that past occurrences will often influence our current and future actions. They don't have to, but this isn't a book about changing your mindsets. The point is that large events will reverberate throughout our entire lives.

So this question will get a response about how people view themselves, for better or worse. Failure will painfully poke perceived flaws they hate about themselves, while achievements will bring up the strengths they are proud of.

A career woman who has worked her way up the corporate ladder might proudly reflect on her accomplishment. Why does she consider this her greatest achievement? Because she values independence, resilience, and determination, and that's exactly what it takes to get to that career pinnacle. She looks back to the things she did in order to get that corner office, and she feels positively about them.

Thus, the answer about her career accomplishments is actually a story about the positive traits she utilized in reaching that point—her self-identity. You can imagine that the same negative type of self-identity might unfold if the same woman were to talk about her failures and ended up in a job that she despised. Those are the exact things she hates the most.

The way that people answer this question shows who they want to be, and this is reflected in exactly how their expectations have either been fulfilled or not.

4. What is effortless and what is always exhausting?

This is a question that is designed to better understand what people actually enjoy. Something that is effortless isn't always an innate talent, but rather an indication that they enjoy it. On the other hand, something that is always exhausting is not always about people's lack of competency, but rather a distaste for the actual activity. Thus, answers to this question can indicate where people find natural joy and enjoyment, even if they don't realize it themselves.

For instance, as a baker answers this question, she may recognize her rather mediocre capacity for creativity for blending ingredients together to make a dessert. Although she is above average, she is not naturally talented at it, and it has been very difficult for as long as she can remember. She was not innately talented with culinary creativity, and yet she finds joy in it such that she is always driven to it. It's challenging but effortless in a way that she doesn't grow tired of.

On the other hand, she may have a natural talent in understanding and following traditional recipes—yet it is not something that she values or particularly cares about. If we were to look at only her innate talents, we would conclude that she should stick to only executing the dishes of others. But it's simply not what she values. As mentioned previously, wherever our time, effort, energy, and money goes, such are our values.

5. If you could design a character in a game, what traits would you emphasize and which would you ignore?

This question asks what people see as their ideal self and also what they feel is less important in the world. Imagine that you have a limited number of points to give a person but six traits to spread the points across. Which will you choose to emphasize and bolster, and which will you choose to leave average or even lacking?

Suppose you have the ability to choose between the traits of charisma, academic intelligence, sense of humor, honesty, resilience, and emotional awareness. The traits you'd choose to put the maximum number of points in is how you'd like others to see you. It may represent your current composition of traits, or it might be completely opposite to who you currently are. In either case, it's more than likely that this either represents how you see yourself or how you would like to see yourself. And the other traits? Well, they simply matter less. In turn, they seek out people with those traits they like and are less keen to seek out those with the other traits. There are probably stories behind each of the traits that people might choose as well.

A related question to ask others is, "What traits are common in other people?" This question comes from a 2010 psychological study by Dustin Wood, in which he found that people tended to describe others with similar traits as themselves. Presumably this is because people tend to see their own qualities in others. No one believes that their mental makeup of traits is uncommon, and thus, they believe everyone has a similar perspective and way of thinking as them. Answers to this question are a direct insight into what traits people believe they have, for better or worse. From there, you know what kind of approach they have to the world—kind, generous, distrusting, mischievous, or even ill-spirited.

6. What charity would you donate millions to if you had to?

Answering this question forces one to answer what they care about in the world at large rather than just in their own life.

Will you donate to an animal shelter or a charity for cancer? Perhaps you would sponsor a child from a third-world country? They all say very different things. You might have had a first- or secondhand experience with any of these causes. Whatever the case, it shows what matters when people start to think outside of themselves. You can see a whole sector of the world that they are concerned about, and this allows you to see how they view their place in the world. In other words, whose interests do they tend to prioritize or be motivated by? As always, look to the underlying emotion.

Being able to ask these questions evokes a deeper connection to people's values, ideas, and awareness. The purpose of asking these is to, again, examine behavior. These questions guide a person in thinking about the most relevant aspects of his or her character. They also make people think beyond predictable statements and organically stimulate more meaningful thought. Look beyond the answers and read between the lines. Critical thinking, evaluation, and reflection are the key skills at play here.

Next, we go deeper by asking people for stories that they construct, rather than just a relatively short answer, to see what we can glean from hearing their internal dialogue in full effect.

7. What animal best describes you?

The great thing about this question is that it's a very personal inquiry hidden in plain sight. People are far more comfortable talking about certain traits they admire in others than they are about talking directly about themselves. You might also find that asking this question has people feeling very willing to share revealing information that they otherwise might have felt too uncomfortable to reveal.

Something about the distance that's created when talking about an animal can prompt some very forthright and honest answers. People may inadvertently tell you about who they *wish* they were when they tell about their favorite animal. Listen carefully to the person who says they love dogs but dislike cats. Ask them why, and their answer will tell you plainly about the traits they value in others, in themselves, and how they wish to be.

The best way to pose this question is as casually as possible. Don't make it seem like you're grilling for a serious answer— ironically, this attitude will quickly reach past people's defenses and have them blurting out information about themselves that can be incredibly meaningful. What they tell you immediately after is important—whatever is top of their mind is the aspect of themselves they likely see as most important, most relevant or most fixed.

For example, a person immediately tells you they're a bear and needs no further prompting for them to explain to you why: they're fierce, protect their loved ones and shouldn't be messed with. But if they didn't choose a shark, could this mean that they also see themselves as having a bit of "cuddly" side to them, too?

On the surface, such questions can seem innocent and playful, but it's this very simplicity that allows people to respond most honestly—as though to a Rorschach test. Did they choose a carnivore or an herbivore? A mythical animal? A pest? A domesticated animal or a wild, slightly dangerous one? Such a question adds immense depth and color to your understanding of the person—and it does so in their own terms.

8. What's your favorite movie?

This is perhaps as obvious on the surface as the previous one, but many people don't stop to truly think about the huge amounts of information they're being offered when people share things like their favorite films. With this question, people are really sharing with you the narratives and stories they're drawn to, which in turn show you in a deep way what their inner moral universe looks like, how they think of the good and bad guys, or even how they envision their own grand story as it unfolds.

What is it about a particular film that they like? Don't simply assume that they identify with the main character—it may be the director or the genre itself that most powerful speaks to them. And if someone answers, "Well, it's a very obscure independent Polish film released in the early 40s. I don't expect you know anything about it," you can infer a lot even though you've never heard of the film! You can assume that this person values exclusivity and rarity, and likes to style themselves a connoisseur with excellent taste (i.e., what other people would identify as an infuriating hipster!).

Use the answer to this question along with other data you're gathering. What does it mean that the shy, skinny kid in the corner best loves a superhero film? What would a retired Japanese mom see in a serious film about the slave trade in the deep south? The person who tells you their favorite film is a comedy—does it mean anything that the comedy they choose is not a recent one, but one from decades past, that would have been popular when they were just a child?

9. What would you rescue from a fire in your home?

You know the drill. Your entire home is burning and you can only go in to fetch one single treasured item, no more. This is another question that taps deeply into a person's most fundamental values and priorities. Maybe you had a particular person pegged as a pragmatic, almost emotionally-stunted person until they tell you they'd save a single book of poetry.

Crisis and emergency situations have a way of quickly cutting through the clutter of life. People may appear a certain way right up until their backs are against the wall. In the film *Force Majeure*, a family finds themselves facing a terrifying but brief threat—an oncoming avalanche. In the few heated moments, the father fleas the scene, saving himself, while the mother stays with her children. Though the danger passes and everyone is soon safe again, the rest of the movie explores what the father's actions mean—did his knee-jerk response in the moment say something about what he really valued—i.e., himself, and not his family?

Try to understand not just what a person would save, but why. A person who would quickly grab their pet cat before anything else is telling you that they value life more than inanimate possessions. A person who grabs their passport is telling you that they see their freedom to move, their ability to travel, as a very special thing.

Similarly, someone who simply tells you they'd grab their wallet because they had all their money, cards and driver's license in there is also telling you something important—that they are interpreting your question not in terms of values or hypotheticals, but as a literal and practical dilemma to be solved in the most logical way possible. Very different from the person who boldly claims they would save an old photograph of their great-great-grandmother!

10. What scares you most?

Many of the above questions are focused on values, principles, priorities, desires. But of course, you can also learn a lot about a person by what they actively avoid, detest and fear. This tells you not only what they do value, but also how they see themselves. After all, it makes sense that you would fear the thing you most felt unable to protect yourself against, or the thing that you felt was most harmful to you personally. This can yield enormous amounts of insight into how a person sees their own strengths and limitations.

Someone who says "spiders" is going to have a very different psychological makeup than someone who claims, "early onset dementia, where I gradually forget who I am and the faces of everyone I used to love." Fears are often a door to people's most firmly held principles—a person who is extremely morally-inclined and driven by justice and fairness might fear serial-killers, psychopaths or even demonic supernatural entities.

On the other hand, fears can also tell you what that person thinks of their ability to handle adversity or suffering. The person who fears rejection, abandonment and criticism is telling you that in their world, psychological harm is more serious than physical harm. Likewise, what would you infer about someone who unflinchingly tells you, "I'm not scared of anything"?

Putting your questions into context

Recall that the idea is to gather *as much* information as possible but also *as many different kinds* of information, so that we can find broad patterns that help us understand people more deeply. Your observations can help you refine targeted questions, and the response to those questions can then be interpreted given the context. Like a scientist, you are testing a provisional theory about the person both with observations and with mini "experiments" (i.e. questions).

Before we move onto the next section, there are a few additional things to observe and question, which can help you enrich your working model and better understand the other person. One method has been called "thin slicing" which is using small amounts of data to make accurate assessments. Snap decisions based on thin slicing can be surprisingly accurate. A good technique is to trust your initial unconscious reactions (intuition) but supplement this with more deliberate observations after the fact.

Note the words people use in their texts and e-mails, for example their use of pronouns, active/passive voice, swearing, accent, word choice and so on. Note how they respond to your emails, which are a form of question. Also note how emotionally charged someone's responses are, and if this amount is appropriate to the context they are used in. For example, using overly negative language in seemingly benign situations can be an indicator of bad mental health or low self-esteem.

Read a person's home and possessions like you would their body language and voice: examine the closedness or openness of a home to determine sociability, for example. Notice what there is an excess of and what is conspicuously lacking in the spaces one occupies frequently. Personal possessions can make identity claims, can speak to the way a person regulates their own emotions, or can be evidence of certain past behaviors or habits. Use them to fine-tune your questions, for example, on seeing a date's home and noticing that there's nothing at all in the fridge, you could guess that the person isn't very domestic, and then you could make an offhand comment like, "oh I'm a real homebody. I love baking especially. In my dreams I have my own cooking show!" Note that this isn't even really a question.. but it functions as one. If the person responds by scoffing and pulling a disgusted microexpression, consider your theory confirmed!

Finally, you can also rely on people's behavior online to discern what kind of person they are, albeit some caution is necessary here. Pay attention to what kind of pictures people post and the emotions they convey, especially whether they are positive, neutral, or negative. Note how people respond online to questions, attention or the lack of it. Many people behave differently online when they believe they are anonymous – is there a big difference between this behavior and their public behavior?

Elicitation

If none of the above work, that's where the practice of *elicitation* comes in. It is a type of directed questioning that uses a specific conversational style to subtly encourage people to share and speak more. It was originally developed by the Federal Bureau of Investigation (FBI) for use during interrogations, but quickly began to be used by corporate spies to obtain confidential information from competitors.

Its origins will probably give you pause; isn't this exactly the type of sneaky, underhanded, and manipulative stuff that we want to avoid? We can see it that way, but in reality, all of these techniques can be used for both good and evil. The techniques themselves are neutral and are a result of taking a look into the human psyche. And remember, we already engage in many sneaky tactics to make people like us— they're just more socially acceptable ones, like wearing makeup or making our job positions sound more significant than they really are.

Elicitation is about understanding the rules that human behavior follows, and then finding clever ways to use those to your advantage. Elicitation, when done right, won't feel like an interrogation.

To use elicitation, you make a statement that plays on the other person's desire to respond for a variety of reasons. The other person will feel driven to respond, even if they had no prior interest in engaging. They will almost feel like they have no choice, or as though they are choosing to respond from their own free will rather than as a response to anything you've said.

As with so many of the other tactics discussed in this book, the art is in being subtle. You need to learn to read between the lines. A direct question will not always get an answer; thus, it becomes important to ask *indirect* questions to encourage opening up.

Here is an example of how elicitation works. You are trying to plan a surprise party for someone, so you need to know his schedule, his friends' contact information, and his food and drink preferences. Of course, you can't ask him for this information directly. So how might you indirectly obtain this information from him?

You might say, "I'm going to buy a grape soda. Do you want one?" This will seem like a random, harmless question, but it can show you his drink preferences when he replies, "Is there root beer?" or, "Sure, grape is fine."

Then you can go on to ask, "My friend is looking for someone to help move. Are you available weeknights at 6 p.m.?" He just might tell you his work schedule as a result: "I'm usually off work at 7 p.m., so I can't help out, sorry."

For a friend's contact, you can say, "Hey, is Josh's phone number 555-5695?" Here, you are intentionally asking him about an incorrect number, which will prompt him to correct it for you: "No, his phone number is actually 555-3958."

You've now obtained three essential pieces of information through indirect means. What's important here is that you've not once aroused any suspicion from your friend, who likely has no clue that you were seeking the kind of information you were. Your goal is to encourage people to volunteer the information on their own, with the smallest and most invisible of prompts. Ellen Naylor in her 2016 book *Win/Loss Analysis* wrote about six specific elicitation techniques to get people talking. Let's take a closer look.

Recognition. Human beings are social animals. We're built for spotting and connecting with people who are like us— we can't help it. This instinct makes us desire approval and acknowledgment, which you can use to effortlessly encourage people to open up.

The idea is simple: people thrive when you recognize something good about them. People cannot help but respond to compliments or kind observations—the more accurate and unusual your observation, the better. Mention, "I love your sweater," and you will get a story about how the wearer obtained the sweater. Mention, "You are very thorough," and you will get a story about how the person went to military school and learned to be thorough at all times.

If you are smart about it, you can pay compliments in a more strategic way. If you are subtly trying to get a person to confess to their real opinion on a subject, you might say something like, "I love how forthright and honest you always are. You speak your mind, and that's a rare thing these days!" You may just nudge them to open up and share what they're *really* thinking. They may have been tight-lipped before, but any chance to enhance praise is welcome—people will usually respond according to the positive feedback they're given, demonstrating the very trait you've observed, or telling you more about their values and beliefs. People have a natural desire to feel recognized and appreciated, so give them an opening to show off a little, or even tell you something you might never have been told if you asked directly.

Simply show appreciation to someone and compliment them. Even if you don't glean some fascinating bit of information from them, you'll still strengthen rapport and learn a little more about them. If you say to a woman, "You're absolutely beautiful! You look like Grace Kelly," and she responds negatively, you know that she doesn't value appearances all that much. Next time round, subtly compliment her intelligence, kindness, or humor, and compare the response. This is similar to recognition; people rarely turn down an opportunity to explain their accomplishments, and they rarely shy away from talking about themselves if asked in the right way.

Complaining. This technique works with something else fundamental to human beings: how much we love to complain! It's easy to get someone to open up by giving them something to commiserate with. Not only will you strengthen the rapport between you and keep things warm and casual, but you'll bond over a "shared enemy" and learn more about the other person.

It's simple. You complain first, and they will jump at the opportunity to join you. If they *don't* join in, they might open up the other way by feeling compelled to defend what you are complaining about. Either way, you've opened them up and learned more about what they care about and who they are.

You might tell someone at work, "I hate these long hours without overtime pay," and he will agree and go into more detail about how he needs money from not being paid enough. This may lead him to disclose more about his home life and how many kids he has and marital issues he has related to finances. It may also lead him to defend the long hours. Either way, you have more information now.

The key to this technique is creating a safe environment for people to brag, complain, or show other raw emotion. The exact topic of the complaint is irrelevant—rather, it's the act of getting people to let their guard down so they can reveal these more genuine emotions. If you complain first, you create a judgment-free zone. You lower your guard a little first. They don't feel like they will get in trouble with you. In fact, they may feel that sharing in kind is simply the polite thing to do, and won't even feel as though they are sharing about themselves at all. You don't have to complain to kickstart this; just express your own negative emotions, vulnerabilities, or disappointments.

"So they say it's going to snow this weekend? Can you believe it? I guess I can put my flip flops away for the time being . . ."

"Aw, it's not so bad! In our house, we call it a *duvet day*. You know—pajamas and something trashy on TV."

"Don't tell me you watch trashy TV!"

"Ah, well, actually . . ."

In just a few exchanges, you're instantly talking about this person's private home life and their personal taste in TV. Much smoother than simply asking, "So, uh, what kind of TV do you watch?"

Correction. The next thing that people really love? People love to be right. When you think about it, this is truly the backbone of any internet argument—it carries on because each party wants to "win." It's not one of humanity's finest habits, true, but the impulse to jump in and put someone right when you *know* they're wrong is a powerful and irresistible one. In other words, if you want people to open up and start talking with emotion, do it by getting them a little riled about something!

If you say something wrong, most people will gladly jump at the chance to correct you. If you give people an opportunity to flex their ego, most will seize it happily. They won't stop there, though—you can also expect to be given a little extra information, too. Notice what specific things the other person seems defensive and passionate about. What does it mean that they don't care if you're wrong about the spelling of a particular word, but will get out the pitchfork if you say something untrue about a mutual friend? Basically, what does their desire to correct, and their correction itself, tell you about their values and personality?

An easy way to practice this technique is to state something you know to be obviously incorrect to see if they will step in and break their silence. See if they can resist this primal urge. The great thing about this is that the other person will certainly not feel coerced or pushed in any way. Instead, they will feel that they are happily supplying information of their own accord.

Imagine a sulky child who won't open up and tell you about what's happened at school that day, although you know *something* happened. The more you ask, the more they clam up.

"Well, that's fine. You don't have to tell me about what happened. It's just strange because I know how much you love Tuesdays because it's PE class, and that's your favorite."

"*What*? It's not my favorite! I *hate* PE. And I *hate* Mrs. Wheeler."

"Mrs. Wheeler? She's that awesome teacher who all the kids love, though, isn't she?"

"No. She isn't. She's horrible, and today she called me stupid in front of the whole class . . ."

Naïveté. In the same vein as the above, many people can't help speaking up when they believe that someone is not wrong exactly, but merely trying to understand, and it's their job to clear things up for them. This principle is used to great effect in what's commonly called the "Columbo technique," which we'll look at in a later chapter. But to be clear, this does not mean acting stupid; it simply means acting like you're on the *cusp* of understanding—and you'll cross that cusp with just a little more explanation from the other person.

Most people love to feel right, and they love to advise, teach, or show the way. Acting naïve makes people feel compelled to teach, instruct, and show off their knowledge to you. People just can't resist enlightening you, especially if you're ninety-five percent of the way there and all people have to do is figuratively finish your sentence. "I understand most of this theory, but there's just this one thing I'm unclear on. It could mean so many things . . ." People won't be able to resist jumping in.

You could frame your confusion as a subtle question, or leave it open-ended so the other person feels compelled to resolve the issue for you.

Use phrases like:

"Okay, so just to get this clear . . ."

"Have I got that right?" (Said after something that isn't wrong, just incomplete.)

"So I know that A is the case, and I know about B, and I can see C, but I'm not seeing the next step." (Said when you want the other person to open up about D.)

Shift the window. This technique is a little more dramatic than the others, and may take a bit more practice, or otherwise being more familiar with the person in question. This is where you say something slightly outrageous that you know won't be answered, then pretend like you didn't bring it up. Why does this work? Does it even work? It works because you have put something out there to dramatically change the tone of the conversation, but then quickly taken it back so it doesn't officially count anymore. Of course, you *have* said it, and they *have* heard it.

The "window" in this case can be thought of as a conversational frame or reference point. You might be having a very serious, guarded conversation with someone, but want to switch the frame, let's say to a more informal, warm, and open one. You can do this by deliberately speaking outside of your current frame, but then backtracking a little or simply leaving your statement or question there to do its work.

Think of it as a cumulative effect—when you do this a couple of times, these are the types of questions people will engage with and answer even if they were ice cold beforehand. You haven't actually committed a faux pas per se, but you've shifted the boundaries of the conversation. It's a good combination that can get people to lower their guards without them even realizing it, and eventually their window of what they feel is appropriate to be shared can shift and widen.

This technique is most commonly seen when people are flirting. Typically, strangers meet one another in a guarded or neutral frame, and the task of the person flirting is to gently nudge this frame to something different entirely. It may take forever if you simply wait for this to happen naturally. But if you throw in a few comments or questions that encourage a different frame, you can gently push the direction of the conversation elsewhere. What's important, though, is that you are never forcing the other person to respond to these frame shifts. Make a subtle shift, and then pull back and watch for the effect. If there is no active resistance or a forceful attempt to regain the previous frame, you can wait a little and try to push a little further next time.

Imagine a conversation where someone is trying to subtly communicate their interest in the other person, and figure out if there is any interest in return. During an ordinary conversation about something unrelated, this person may slip in a few frame-shifting comments and questions like:

"What a great idea. You see? That's why you're my favorite."

"What do you think of this shirt, though? You're a fashion forward kind of person; would you date someone who wore a shirt like this?"

"Oh, don't say that! And here I thought we had a little thing going."

Subtle frame shifts can also be used by therapists who are trying to shift an avoidant client around to discussing difficult feelings, or by anyone who wants to gently broach a delicate topic, like money.

"I've noticed we've been carefully avoiding talking about this issue with your mother . . ."

Even if the other person doesn't respond to this invitation to shift frames, they will have heard what you said, and may, in time, come around. Given minutes after this comment, for example, a reluctant person may randomly tell their therapist, "I know I keep avoiding talking about her. I guess I'm feeling pretty uncomfortable right now."

Silence. This last technique may not seem like the others, but in many cases, it can be the most powerful of all. Here, we have to counter our own innate tendency to talk all the time and control the conversation. Instead, simply give people space to speak. Stop talking, and allow a quiet moment to open up inside the conversation.

When you take a step back, people will feel compelled to take a step forward and break the awkward tension. We have all been taught that it's "our turn" to speak in conversations when the other person stops and goes silent. If you signal that you expect someone to speak and are waiting for them, they may open their mouths to meet your expectations, just to keep the dialogue going. They might not immediately tell you what you want to know, but at least they're talking again.

On the other hand, some people may be holding back because they feel unsure or don't want to be judged. They may literally just need the time it takes to gather their thoughts and speak through them. If the other person is continually talking, they may feel like they never get the chance. Again, it's about being subtle and encouraging people to talk to you on *their* terms. You can try any of the techniques above and end them with a moment of silence to give the other person a full chance to respond.

If you talk too much yourself, or jump in immediately after you've made a comment or question, the other person might sense that you have an agenda and that you're trying to dominate the conversation—and clam up. Instead, use silence to communicate a few things: that you're listening (non-judgmentally), that you're interested in what they have to say, and that you are in effect waiting for them to say it. A silence is like an invitation. It's like asking the other person, "What do you want to fill this with?"

Notice the other person's body language. The worst thing you can do is blurt out something just as they were about to speak. One way to hold silences is not to just sit and watch the other person expectantly, but rather make it comfortable. Make it seem like you are happy to talk, but also okay with not talking. Communicate with your tone of voice and body language that you are not especially invested in them saying anything—but that you are there should they decide to say it! This takes the pressure off them and makes it easier for them to speak up.

To conclude, asking questions and eliciting information are best practiced alongside more passive observation techniques. If you observe something interesting, think of a question to pose to help you focus in on that observation and gain more insight. Working in tandem, observation and elicitation are like the active and passive poles of the same process. When they both inform and guide one another, you will be orders of magnitude more effective at extracting information than if you'd used either one on its own.

Takeaways

- Asking questions is an active way to deliberately elicit information from a person, but they need to be targeted and not too obvious. A few seemingly casual hypothetical questions can reveal a person's deeper values, perspectives and goals, for example asking what their favorite movie is, what they would save from a fire, or what animal they see themselves as.
- Analyze the answers to these questions cautiously, and remember to place everything in context. Note *how* they answer, not just the content, and also not what isn't said. Use extrapolation to draw conclusions about what their answers say about them in a more general sense.
- Questions needs to be iterative and responsive to the context and the answers you've already received. Also think about behavior online and in

emails, or "read" a person's possessions or home the way you would their body language. Use these observations to guide your questions.

- Elicitation is more deliberate still, and uses a string of guiding questions to lead a person to give you precisely the information you're looking for, without it seeming that you are.
- Developed originally by the FBI, these techniques are really just ways to carefully work around conversational and societal norms to your advantage. They are effective because they work with human being's natural social and behavioral tendencies.
- For example, one tendency is towards recognition, or social connection. Use compliments or accurate observations to foster a rapport with someone or strengthen your connection.
- You can also elicit information by encouraging people to complain, and in doing so, reveal something previously hidden, or else tap into the human need to correct someone's error. Sued skillfully, most people cannot resist

joining in on a complaining session or correcting an "error" you make.

- Playing dumb or using naivete or ignorance will also encourage some people to try to educate you, and share vital information, especially since you will seem so non-threatening.
- Finally, one technique is to say something quite dramatic to "shift the window" and then act as though nothing has happened; subtly, you may well elicit a revealing response. Silence can also be used effectively, since it encourages people to fill the gap with the information you want to know.

Chapter 3. Comfort

We've been painting a picture of human beings as dynamic, responsive agents in a constantly shifting environment. We can observe them and their environment, and make inferences and educated guesses about who they are, as well as use indirect questions to subtly confirm our suspicions or reveal deception. But one way to elicit information that you might not have thought of is to work not on the person themselves, but on the environment they're in. It's a subtle shift, but it comes down to creating an atmosphere of trust and comfort.

Some people start with zero trust in strangers and keep their guards high until they see enough signs that they feel comfortable letting their guard down. For these people, trust is slowly earned and a privilege, never a given. Trust is the ultimate placing of faith in someone, and that's not something to be taken lightly.

On the other hand, other people immediately embrace strangers with open arms and assume good intentions. This is where trust is automatically given as a policy, with the understanding that it can be lost.

Wherever you might fall on that spectrum, it's clear that trust is assigned different values based on people's experiences. If you've had positive experiences with being open with strangers, you're more likely to continue in that fashion, and vice versa. This is all to say that trust can be a hard quality to nail down, perhaps harder than other facets of likability and charm.

But is there a way to shortcut the process if you come across someone who thinks trust is to be earned over a long period of time? How can you win over even the most guarded and standoffish person who doesn't even leave their bag with you when they use the restroom?

Well, on the topic of direct trust alone, there is a multitude of studies about what compels that feeling. A 2018 study called "Stimulus Generalization as a Mechanism for Learning to Trust" by Oriel FeldmanHall found that trust we feel toward others depends on if the person resembles a past individual that was either trustworthy or untrustworthy. This would imply that trust functions more like what made Pavlov's dog salivate—a kneejerk reaction based on a simple association. For a more conventional perspective, a 1985 publication called "Trust in Close Relationships" by Rempel, Holmes, and Zanna found that trust requires reliability, predictability, and thinking that the other person is concerned with your feelings. However, one of the first landmark studies on trust provides a more interesting and perhaps indirect insight into what creates trust, and it's one that we can harness for likability as well.

More Is Better

Festinger, Schachter, and Back studied the concept of trust in 1950 in "Social Pressures in Informal Groups: A Study of Human Factors in Housing." They studied people who lived in an apartment building and the patterns of the friendships that formed. They found that neighbors who were on the same floor tended to be friends, people who lived on different floors were rarely friends, and people who lived near the mailboxes and staircases were friends with people on different floors.

What can we conclude from this?

To a large extent, friendship and trust increase *linearly* with simple interaction and exposure. The more we see someone, the more likely we will become friends with them and come to trust them. It didn't matter if there was any depth or rapport. The amount of interaction was the only factor that appeared to matter in the study. This was dubbed *the propinquity effect*.

On a practical level, the more we see people, the more we interact with them, the more similarities we find, the more comfort we build, and the more we find that we can potentially like them. People cease to be whatever stereotype you have in mind, and they turn into unique, two-dimensional humans. This is something we'll cover in greater detail in a later chapter on how to avoid negative judgments.

Prolonged exposure by itself will embed people into your mind as essentially part of the background. This is why when we change schools, jobs, or homes, we miss our neighbors or coworkers, even if we rarely spoke to them. There has been so much exposure and interaction that we tend to view them in a positive light and associate them with the environment as a whole. The level of interaction itself isn't important; the frequency of the interaction is.

The propinquity effect is why it's not surprising that we are frequently friends with roommates, neighbors, coworkers, and classmates. You have a high level of exposure and interaction, you let your guard down around them, and you create an open mind toward friendship. If you look at your set of close friends, you would realize that a lot of those friends became friends of yours almost accidentally. They just frequently showed up in your life. They were at the right place at the right time and they did the same things you did. You struck up a conversation, and then you kept seeing each other on a regular basis.

It turns out that half of the battle in likability is *showing up* and not hiding in your room like a cat. The more you show your pretty face, the more trust will ultimately be built. For those you are specifically targeting to make friends and build trust with, make sure to frequently bump into them. The interaction itself can be minimal, as long as they take notice of your presence and acknowledge you. The goal is to become a known and familiar quantity in their lives.

This manifests in even tiny ways in our daily life. The more you see a certain barista at a café you frequent, the more you feel like you know and trust them. The more you see a neighbor, even if it's just while you are both taking out your trash, the more you feel like you understand who they are and trust them. Repetition creates trust.

A stark illustration of the importance of frequency of exposure is in sales. This is known sometimes as the sales or marketing rule of seven, which states that a customer needs to see a product or hear the product's pitch at least seven times in order to be ready to purchase. Another advertising guide written by Thomas Smith in 1885 espouses the need for 20 separate *touchpoints* before a purchase is made.

In addition, salespeople are taught that the sale is always made in the follow-up and not the initial contact, and the propinquity effect is part of the reason why. So they will email, call, text, and make sure that you have so many points of contact with them that they are always in your ear.

And oddly enough, this makes you trust them more because of the frequency and duration of their presence—if nothing has gone wrong or terribly, then they are slowly proving themselves to be trustworthy, right?

If you are trying to get people to like you and become their friend, the same process applies. Obviously, adopt a subtler method, but it's undeniable how salespeople are able to gain our trust through repeated exposure and interaction.

The propinquity effect is highly related to the *mere exposure effect*, which similarly states the more we see something, the more we like it because we prefer familiarity. In 1968 in "Attitudinal Effects of Mere Exposure," researcher Robert Zajonc showed participants Chinese characters— some characters only once and some up to 25 times. He asked them to guess the meaning of each character, and the more times a participant had been exposed to the Chinese character, the more positive of a meaning they assigned to it.

These various effects demonstrate that things tend to grow on us, and sometimes our tastes arise out of exposure and familiarity, not free will or actual affection. Familiarity is the ultimate precursor to trust.

Credibility

Credibility can be seen as a higher degree of trust. If you trust someone, you believe them but may not be sure about their sense of judgment. You feel comfortable that they care about you. However, if you believe someone has *credibility*, you may not necessarily trust them, but you view their judgment as rock-solid. You believe what they say, though you might feel differently about their character. It might be a personal preference as to which of the two is more important, but it'd be even better to be able to create the feeling of both.

Scientifically speaking, there is a wealth of subtle signs that can either bolster someone's credibility or tank it. If you've had any media training, or simply watched a politician interact with the media, you'll know that credibility doesn't just happen by accident. There are specific behaviors that make us want to believe them; they signal that this person is dependable, isn't a threat, and should in fact be followed.

It's a finely tuned science that can make or break people. As recently as 1999, Gass and Seiter in their book *Persuasion, Social Influence, and Compliance Gaining* sought to study credibility. They discovered a host of subtle indicators of credibility, as well as a host of signs that undermined credibility.

Here are the signs that need to be in play for people to think you're credible.

Highlight your experience and your qualifications. People are looking for an indication that you know what you're talking about. At the very least, they want to see facts that would support a conclusion that whatever judgments or decisions you make are based on something real. This is important for most people because if you've already seen something in the past or have been educated about it, chances are you know the right things to do. You would have the right information so the right decisions are made. People want proven quantities and not just people making educated guesses.

Display how much you care. If it's obvious you care about other people and have their best interests at heart, they are more likely to trust you. You simply wouldn't act in any other way except to help them. However, if people can sense that you're looking to get a sale or line your own pockets, they are less likely to trust you. There is a conflict of interest here. They might feel that you are just too busy trying to benefit yourself instead of actually looking out for them. Don't show any ulterior motives, and let people know you are on their side.

Similarity. You already know this. When people see that you are similar to them in terms of dress, body language, speaking style, and mother tongue, they are more likely to view you as credible. People tend to like other people who are like them. This is especially true if it appears that you share the same values as the people you're trying to impress. They'll believe you because people automatically trust those similar to them, such as their family.

Appear assertive. If you are very assertive regarding your positions and you quickly and rationally destroy counterarguments, this makes you look like an expert. This is passion and conviction and confidence. This means that you know what you're talking about—or at least you look like you do. Chances are people can trust your judgments because you know the other side of the argument and can convincingly make those arguments go away. In other words, the more decisively you act, the more credible you appear.

Gain social proof. When other credible people recommend you, chances are people will be less suspicious of you. If people they know and trust as experts recommend you, then you are essentially riding on the coattails of those people. You don't have to convince people because people they trust already opened the doors for you. This is an extremely important competitive advantage. Unfortunately, not everybody can tap into this. This is what's behind every warm introduction. People will take a chance on you because someone vouched for you, and that's a powerful statement.

Likewise, there are certain signals you can send out that can erode your credibility.

Don't contradict yourself. If you are caught telling a lie or an obvious exaggeration, this can vaporize whatever credibility you've built up. If you're unsure about a certain assertion, follow this simple rule: when in doubt, leave it out. People may ask questions, and in many cases, you may not have answers to those questions. Instead of trying to look like a hero and guessing at an answer, you would be better off telling people you don't know or you'll get back to them. Recognize that you don't need an answer for everything, and if you appear infallible, it can look suspicious or manipulative. If you don't appear stupid, you might appear to be lying.

Avoid being overly polite. This might come as a surprise to some. By being excessively polite and brownnosing, you can come off as weak and tentative, which means that your opinions will also be taken as such. You look like you are simply looking for approval and telling people what they want to hear. You also appear to be insincere and manipulative, even if you are being sincere and honest. Too much politeness can often belie a lack of conviction or stance. You have to remember that people are looking for others whom they can listen to and follow. If you are busy walking on eggshells around them, you're sending the wrong signals.

For many, the initial reaction to these credibility factors will be that they apply to an office environment. For instance, you might pay special attention to them during a job interview and not apply them in social situations. It may seem that way, but appearing credible to friends—the feeling that they rely on you and believe in your judgment—is just as important socially. It just shifts you into a person that others will listen to instead of ignore. And of course, credibility and trust work hand in hand to increase your likability.

Look into My Eyes

We've saved what is probably the most intuitive indicator of trust for the end of the chapter.

Surely, you've heard many times before that eye contact is *important*. *Eyes are the window to the soul, you can tell someone's goodness just by looking them in the eye, he wouldn't look at me in the eye and lie*, and so on. If you look up advice on dating, job interviews, sales, or just making friends, sustained eye contact will no doubt make the list as a key to what you want. We believe eyes convey emotion and empathy and that we can literally feel it from others when we lock eyes.

As a society, we place a lot of value on the implications of eye contact and what it means for trust in particular. If you meet someone who refuses to meet your eye contact, or conversely meets it for too long, you feel discomfort and leave with a negative impression of that person. People who don't make eye contact are perceived as being untrustworthy or deceitful. This ages-old assumption has been disproven repeatedly, most recently in 2012 in "The Eyes Don't Have It: Lie Detection and Neuro-Linguistic Programming" by Wiseman and Watt, which found no correlation between eye contact and deceit but instead a considerable correlation between hand gestures and deceit.

So while the lack of eye contact doesn't *actually* say anything about others, it may as well be true if people make those assumptions about you.

On the other hand, there is a truly significant number of positive assumptions that we make about people who make eye contact and that can surely improve people's perception of you. Generally, people who make eye contact are seen as more dominant and powerful; warmer and more personable; more attractive and likable; more qualified, skilled, competent, and valuable; more trustworthy, honest, and sincere; and more confident and emotionally stable. In other words, just about all the things that are associated with social success.

Why do we care so much about eye contact or the lack thereof? Is it just because we have been told from childhood to look at people in the eye and give them a firm handshake? Of course, it turns out that what may have started as old-fashioned advice from an older generation truly has many scientific confirmations.

In 1978 in "Effects of Eye Contact and Social Status on the Perception of a Job Applicant in an Employment Interviewing Situation," Tessler and Sushelsky found that we tend to make positive or negative assumptions based on how much someone meets our eye gaze—the more, the better.

In 2001 in "Accurate Intelligence Assessments in Social Interactions: Mediators and Gender Effects," Murphy and Hall found that we generally consider those who return eye contact to be more intelligent, conscientious, and sincere.

In 2016 in "Direct Speaker Gaze Promotes Trust in Truth-Ambiguous Statements," Kreysa and Kressler found that more eye contact promotes feelings of trust and genuineness.

Oddly enough, you probably knew the outcomes of these studies already. Whether they represent the truth or are just assumptions, we have to make sure that we don't fall on the wrong side of those studies.

As we are increasingly more caught up in a battle for our attention between our phones and our real-life conversation partners, the ability to make eye contact has become an especially powerful tool. When you can utilize eye contact smartly to show somebody that they have your undivided attention, you can effectively win them over and enhance their perception of you.

There was never a need to convince you about the role of eye contact in trust, but there is one rather large caveat with eye contact—how should we use it? We can't simply stare into someone's eyes and try to read their souls. That is extremely uncomfortable and unsettling. In fact, eye contact has been shown to consume a significant amount of our brainpower and focus when we utilize it.

A 2016 Japanese study by Kajimura and Nomura titled "When We Cannot Speak: Eye Contact Disrupts Resources Available to Cognitive Control Processes During Verb Generation" found that eye contact consumes a significant portion of our general cognitive resources, and it is difficult to perform other actions, even talking, when making focused eye contact. If this is true for us, it is true for the person you are speaking to. Sustained eye contact is uncomfortable and causes a special kind of internal tension. This is probably why we feel the need to break eye contact when we want to remember something or explain something more complex. Give people a break.

In fact, in 2006, in a paper titled "Helping Children Think: Gaze Aversion and Teaching" by Phelps and Doherty-Sneddon, researchers found that kids told to look away while thinking and solving problems showed a 20% increase in performance.

So how can we improve our eye contact to create feelings of trust? It has to start from the scientific evidence that people feel uncomfortable with a lot of sustained eye contact, but they also feel that you are a shady character if you don't provide enough. Where is the thin line where you are making your best impression and being most likable?

In 2016, Binetti and Hanson investigated the question of the average preferred length of eye contact. In "Pupil Dilation as an Index of Preferred Mutual Gaze Duration," they found that the average preference was only three seconds (before breaking contact and reengaging later). Most people preferred something between two to five seconds, and no one preferred anything under one second or over nine seconds. The thin line of eye contact appears to be that as long as you hold it for three seconds at a time, more often than not, then you will be seen as trustworthy. More eye contact is not better. Not even close to it.

In 1975 in "Eye-Contact, Distance, and Affiliation," Argyle and Dean observed that people tend to maintain eye contact roughly 40–60% of the time when conversing, and we should seek to maintain eye contact for 80% of the time. This leads us to my personal guidelines: make eye contact 50% when talking and 75% when listening.

When you speak, you want others to be comfortable having their attention on you, but you also want to make sure that you don't appear to be hiding something or feeling uncomfortable yourself. And as you listen, you want whoever is speaking to see that you are engaged, but you don't want to look at them so much that they might feel creeped out. As long as you are in the general ballpark of 50% and 75% for speaking and listening, respectively, you'll be making the most out of the surprisingly powerful tool of eye contact.

Listening

Active listening is one of the strongest relationship-building skills you can have in your arsenal. It's also a set of tools that you can use to help you better understand people, and extract the information you want from them. It establishes respect and concern for your partner's viewpoints and makes it easier for you to process information that's intricate and difficult to understand through passive listening. It also eases the communication process: active listening helps you learn what the other person's needs are, and therefore makes you less cautious and more open with your responses.

Perhaps above all else, active listening makes it 100 percent clear and certain that you *are* comprehending your conversation partner. They know that you're right there with them. It's not rocket science – people share more with others they genuinely like and trust, and who they feel are actually listening.

At the same time, we have to push our ego out of the way so we can truly access what the other person is saying. We call this process "active" listening because it engages so many parts of our mind and makes us *do* something to understand what's being communicated.

Therapists (good ones, at least) are excellent models of how to be an active listener. They listen to their clients with a clear purpose. If there's something they're hearing that they're not 100 percent sure about, they encourage their clients to be clear and deliberate.

These therapists try to restate their patients' statements and ask them to elaborate on what they mean. Above all, they try to make their clients feel calm and safe about communicating through contemplation, clear body language, and a spirit of empathy. Therapists are driven by a very clear goal of hearing their clients out, and their every response is informed by this goal. Can we say the same about ourselves when we are trying to listen to others?

You might get carried away with all sorts of convoluted techniques to get a person to reveal a deception or spot how they really feel, or, you might actually have more success genuinely befriending that person so that they *want* to open up to you – no fancy FBI techniques needed!

The listening methods we'll look at in this section are great for anyone who wants to improve their relationships and their communication skills, as well as become better in general at conversation. But they are also a subtle yet effective way of creating an environment that will make people psychologically comfortable. From there, many of the interrogation techniques we've discussed may not even be necessary.

Granted, not everyone has the time to foster an authentic and rich relationship with the people they want to understand better, but if possible, try to work in some of the following principles when dealing with those you're trying to extract information from.

Active listening involves a few essential types of reactions and inquiries that you can start using almost immediately. These are all designed to ensure that the speaker can *feel* you are on the same emotional page as them. After all, what's listening if it's only going on inside your head, and not being conveyed to the other person?

Comprehending. The first step in active listening is, of course, comprehending what the other person is saying in the first place. If the person who's talking to us is speaking the same language as we normally do, this process is fairly automatic.

But there are other potential blocks—for example, if the person uses a lot of jargon or slang that we aren't familiar with or if there are differences in generation, social standing, or culture that we just don't know enough about. Above all else, you just want to make sure you are on the same emotional page as the speaker, so you can ascertain their needs and desires at the moment.

A great thing to ask if we're not understanding what someone's saying is *"Can you explain it to me as if I were five years old?"* A five-year-old knows enough words to hold a conversation but needs to have relatively complex situations described to them in a very patient, deliberate way using the words they already know. Especially if you think the other person fears appearing condescending or patronizing, asking them to describe something as if you were, let's say, *far younger than your actual age,* can make them feel a little more at ease.

Other statements to ask for help comprehending include:

- "What happened?"

- "Tell me your story."

- "What do you mean?"

- "Tell me more."

- "Can you clear this part up for me?"

Don't be afraid of coming across as stupid or interrupting. Most people like to feel like experts, and we are all experts in our own experience. It can even be useful sometimes to be completely transparent about your lack of understanding—if you frame this as a reason for you to listen all the more closely so you can learn!

Retaining. More than just remembering what you just heard, retaining information is hearing what the speaker is trying to say so we can give back a suitable reply. You're trying to get the whole story here, and this goes far beyond simple facts and events. The goal is to place yourself in the speaker's shoes as closely as possible, and of course, questions are necessary for that.

When we're listening to someone, we tend to retain only the details that strike us more personally or in ways that we're most used to retaining information. But that's only our lens, and not particularly useful for trying to be a better listener.

For example, if someone's telling us about a date they went on, we might be the kind who remembers the physical details of the event (what restaurant they went to, what movie they saw, what they were wearing). Or we might recall some more general narrative about the date as a whole (what personality the other person had, what the date "felt like," how it compared to other dates in the past).

We might not even notice ourselves picking out pieces of the narrative that push our buttons, and internally we can set to work constructing a slightly different story for ourselves than the one we're being offered. You might have been on the receiving end of this, when you tell someone something as they seem only to latch on to one aspect of the story that definitely wasn't your focus. Its definitely a way to "listen without listening"!

In conversation we generally look for openings for us to say something and "get our two cents in." This is normal, but it's not conducive to active listening. To properly retain what our conversation partner is telling us, we have to put our egos away and focus squarely on the other person's words, as they are laying them out. It's not about your interpretation, but theirs.

Again, questions are a powerful tool to frame things and keep your focus on the other person's expression. To ensure you're retaining all the relevant information you need, you could ask:

- "What does that mean to you?"

- "And just to be clear, what happened after?"

- "Wait, how did she approach that?"

- "How does that figure into the story?"

- "How did that make you feel?"

- "What was your reaction?"

Responding. Active listening requires an effort to form a knowing and proper response—otherwise, the speaker might feel like they're talking to a brick wall. As has been said multiple times, listening is anything *but* passive! An effective response will demonstrate our concern for what our conversation partner is talking about.

You're listening, comprehending, and retaining already; a quality response will prove that you *understand* everything the speaker has said and picked up on their nonverbal communication. Imagine that you are speaking to someone, and you're not sure that they understand the language you are speaking. They give no indication of comprehension—do you feel listened to? That's why a response is necessary.

Like retaining, it's important that a response isn't tinted with our own ego or ideas. You don't want to respond in ways that suggest you're trying to steer, manipulate or interpret the conversation according to your own agenda. You're trying to get a sense of the other person's feelings and opinions without biases you've developed:

> *Speaker A:* And that's why I don't like going to dinner parties.

Respondent B: That sounds insane! Were you flustered when that odd man jumped out of the cake?

Speaker A: Not flustered so much as disappointed. I expected something a little more grown-up from the Temperance League.

Respondent B: It must have tried your patience. Did it?

Speaker A: A little bit. But more than anything else, it just proved that I have to start putting some restrictions on the entertainment budget.

Responses in active listening should be reflective of what the speaker has said. They should display a deep interest in your partner's thoughts and feelings. Rather than expressing our *own* opinions and viewpoints, good responses in active listening help both parties make their own self-discoveries.

In issuing a quality response, try to reply to your partner's thoughts and feelings—the factual content is often less relevant than it first appears. You can do this by restating what they've said in your own words. Stay within their standpoint when you respond; introducing a suggestion or idea that doesn't have anything to do with their immediate situation could be too jarring or distracting. Don't offer a contradictory or conflicting opinion until you have fully understood, as much as you can, everything your partner is conveying to you. And even then, try to keep strong judgments tamped down.

Some positive responses in active listening might be:

- "I'm intrigued by your story."

- "That sounds like a ____ situation."

- "I can see how you'd feel that way."

- "I get the sense that you feel something has to change—what would you like to see happen?"

- "Do you feel ____ about this situation?"

The general goal of active listening is to fully grasp the viewpoint or life experience of the person who's speaking to you, and for you to absorb that information in a meaningful way that could spur you to new knowledge and understanding. You want to show the other person that you can step inside their world and see their experience from their point of view. To accomplish the goals of comprehending, retaining, and responding, you can employ a few or more of these techniques:

Restating. Paraphrasing your partner's sentiments in your own words is an exceptional way to facilitate your comprehension. It's important *not* to simply repeat what they said back to them like a parrot, but rather to show that you've caught the essence of what they were expressing. You'll recognize this as a kind of "support response" discussed earlier. You're letting them know that you heard them and are on the same page with them. If you're not 100 percent right, they will almost certainly be sure to correct you.

> *Them:* That situation confused and scared me.

> *You:* It must have felt like a dangerous moment—it must have been hard to know what to do.

Reflecting. An alternative way of restating is to frame your reply along the lines of emotions rather than events or story points. Reflecting gives the speaker's story a deeper level that you can prove you have a handle on. Literally tell them, or ask them, about the emotion they are experiencing.

> *Them:* So in the end, my dad said he knew all along I wouldn't get into that college.

> *You:* That's terrible. That sounds like a cruel kind of rejection.

Summarizing. Try to verbally round up the details of a speaker's story into a concise form that displays your grasp of the whole picture. This is similar to restating, but you are going for a broader overview. You can also treat this as a test for your understanding. Many points and arguments may have been stated, and you may have lost sight of the primary emotion, action, or purpose.

> *You:* So the baker got your order wrong, the dinner was burned, and they sent a hypnotist instead of a clown. Man, if that were *my* kid's birthday party, I'd feel ticked off!

Label emotions. Often, a speaker will get lost in the practical and physical details of what they're relating to you. As sensitively as possible, try to identify the emotions they haven't been able to specifically verbalize yet. This is not inherently difficult to do, as you only have to state a type of positive or negative feeling, but when you accurately label someone's emotion, you are going to be seen as a psychic. Just watch out that you're not overreaching or trying to inject your own ideas into the matter.

> *Them:* Finally my boss apologized for overlooking my work and assured me that he was going to pay more attention from now on.

> *You:* Wow, I'm guessing you feel pretty relieved and vindicated by that—not to mention a little cocky.

Probing. Without sounding like an invasive interrogator, try to ask leading questions that will elicit a deeper level of understanding and meaning from the person you're speaking with. Most people enjoy being asked questions that are well-formed and not too presumptuous. When you probe, you can try to make guesses at how people feel, their reactions and desires. This type of forecasting shows that you are so engaged you want to jump to conclusions with them, and keep riding their train of thought. You're not only there with them, you're caught up in their emotions.

> *You:* What did it feel like when that woman berated your kid at the supermarket? How did you *really* want to respond?

Silence. Frequently there's more to be said by a well-placed silence than by filling up the space with additional verbiage. Silence can give every participant a miniature moment of time to gather themselves and their thoughts. It could also help reduce the tension that could arise from a heated or fruitless interaction.

> *Them:* And *that's* when I decided skydiving wasn't my thing, especially when it's work-related.

> *You:*

Not *sermonizing, giving unsolicited advice, or glibly reassuring.* Nobody likes to be put on a level secondary to someone else, and in communication, this might make the speaker feel like shutting down further discussion.

> *Them:* And worst of all, he cannot remember to put the toilet seat down.

> *Sermonizing you:* You should never have let him in your bathroom in the first place.

> *Unsolicited advising you:* You should barricade the bathroom until he agrees to your demands.

> *Glibly reassuring you:* Don't worry about it! Tomorrow's another lovely day full of wonderful possibilities.

Asking leading and open-ended questions. To show that you're invested in your partner's well-being, ask some nonbinary questions about their experience. These questions show that you're ready to get input and that you're interested in more than just the data or facts of a certain situation.

> *Them:* So I decided, a couple hundred dollars later, perhaps parallel parking was something we were going to have to work a little harder on.

> *You:* How does that make you feel? What are your plans for learning? Where do you plan on doing it? What do you hope comes out of it?

Active listening takes a lot of patient work and practice and can even be challenging for people who are good at it. But it pays off in creating an atmosphere of true comprehension, easier information flow, and increased respect for all parties. What we are trying to do, albeit systematically, with active listening is to catch the habit of being conscious of other people's emotions and suppressing our own. The ultimate form of this comes in empathetic reflection.

At this point, you may be feeling a little uneasy about using human being's natural desire for connection and the pretense of empathy to gather information. Rest assured that using active listening is one of the *least* underhanded ways to get into the heads of people around you. In fact, you and everyone you know probably already does it to some extent, albeit unconsciously.

The techniques covered in this chapter – active listening, using eye contact, building trust and credibility – are best suited to situations when you want people to confide in you, open up about a secret or share their true feelings. Think of them as ways to create more intimacy, and remove barriers to sharing information. Naturally, it's a bad move to foster closeness and trust only to gather information to harm somebody, or catch them out. In the case of detecting deception or finding out deliberately hidden information, however, you may find the techniques covered in the final chapter of this book more applicable (and more ethical!).

Takeaways

- Trust has been shown to work in a linear fashion. The more you see someone, the more you trust them, regardless of interaction or depth. This is known as the propinquity effect, and can be used to your advantage in making people feel psychologically comfortable with sharing more with you.
- Credibility is a notch above trust; trust is about people feeling that they can believe you, and credibility is where people also feel that they can rely on you. There are also proven ways to create an aura of credibility around yourself. These include highlighting qualifications, showing your caring and empathy, showing similarity, being assertive, showing social proof, not

contradicting yourself, and avoiding being overly polite.

- Eye contact is essential for building trust. If you aren't able to use eye contact, people will find you untrustworthy. The optimal eye contact period is around three seconds of eye contact at a time, with sufficient rest between gazes.

- Active listening is a valuable skill set that any person should master, but the techniques of active listening can also help you improve your elicitation abilities and gather more information about people. You need to comprehend, retain and respond to the information people are sharing with you.

- You can build rapport and connection in many ways, for example by restating, reflecting, summarizing, labeling emotions, probing (gently!) and using silence to encourage the other person to open up. Open-ended or leading questions (like those covered in the previous chapter) can subtly guide a person to open up to you.

- Avoid giving advice, lecturing, sermonizing or judging.
- Active listening techniques are best used when you would like someone to open up with you and share their true feelings. Other techniques are more appropriate for detecting deception.

Chapter 4. Read and Tell

So far, this book has been about ways to extract information from people without them being aware that you're doing it. With the power of observation and a few targeted questions, you can read far more into people than what they believe they're sharing with you. And so, in this spirit of developing a special kind of listening for things that aren't said outright, we have to take a look at those people who have thoroughly mastered this skill: con artists.

More specifically, we'll look closely at the techniques employed by those claiming to be psychics, mystics, mediums, and clairvoyants who can hear the voice of your dead auntie. Now, two points before we continue: first, we won't discuss the truth of the claims made by such people, i.e. whether it is or isn't possible to tell the future, hear the dead, or read minds, and leave this to your own discretion.

Second, the point of learning these techniques is not to become a TV show charlatan wearing beads and going into trances. Rather, we will take a look at how the methods used in this admittedly cheesy phenomenon can actually be used more universally. In other words, if we want to learn a few more techniques for reading people well, the fake psychics have a lot to teach us.

So-called cold-reading techniques are a little more advanced than the clues and signs we've learned about in earlier chapters, and require us to think on our feet and adapt pretty quickly in evolving situations. But the great thing about cold reading is that it can be done, well, *cold*, i.e. without you ever having met the person before. With practice, you can combine many of the techniques already discussed (such as body language, clothing, mannerisms, etc.) with cold reading to make it even more powerful.

The essence of cold reading is that you are guessing. Nothing mystical or magical, just guessing. The trick, however, is to make guesses in such a way that it seems like you *aren't* guessing. Usually, you make a guess that has a high probability of being right, and then closely observe the result, altering your strategy as you go according to the information you're given. A good cold reader also hurries on so quickly from wrong guesses, and the audience barely notices he was wrong because he's busy weaving new connections and links, and emphasizing his "hits."

Cold reading works because it is a very ordinary, obvious practice that is cleverly camouflaged to *seem* quite mysterious and unlikely. To show you what I mean, let me cold read you right now! Imagine that I have the paranormal gift that allows me to psychically examine the readers of this book, to reach out supernatural tendrils and connect to your inner-most feelings. Ah, now I see you! This is what I see:

You have recently experienced some change but are doing your best to adapt. You're a complex person with many things you don't tell others, although when you are close to someone, you are open and enjoy good company. You sometimes feel a little socially anxious, and worry about mistakes you've made in the past. You are unique and quite different from most other people. Sometimes, you're fearful of the future. Though you like novelty and excitement, you also do appreciate time to rest.

Chances are, all of the above applies to you, dear reader. But it's not magic. Why? Because this description applies to almost *everyone.* The above is the perfect example of a high-probability guess that is broad enough to have some "hits" when offered to a complete stranger.

If I could be in the room with you right now, I could have subtly tweaked this description to include things I noticed about you—your facial expression, age, gender, accent—to make the guess appear even more accurate. Maybe I notice you're wearing a T-shirt with a political slogan on it. Maybe you say something like, "Well, I guess it *is* true that I'm not much like other people . . ." Or maybe you merely smile when I allude to your individuality in my description. Maybe

I notice that you're young, female, outspoken, and have an uncommon accent you seem to be trying to conceal. I put all of this together and know instantly what to focus on in the rest of my "reading."

It's easy to create the impression of supernatural gifts or intuition if you want to, but you can use cold-reading techniques more benignly to gather huge amounts of information from others. Why not use it to learn more about the people around you, or to create rapport and a feeling of connection? Perhaps without knowing it, people like psychologists and other helping professionals also use a little cold reading to quickly get to know the people in front of them! Good cold reading uses several of the techniques we'll consider in a moment, as well as the powerful observational and listening skills we've already discussed.

If possible, try to prepare beforehand. Fraudulent psychics will secretly spy on the crowd or specially select a group known for their suggestibility. For our purposes, you can prepare by learning as much about your "audience" ahead of time. If you can't, simply consider the context and what it might mean for the people you'll encounter. For a very obvious example, if you encountered a youngish couple at a baby fair one weekend, you might reasonably infer that they were attempting to have a baby or were already pregnant.

Technique 1: Shotgun Statements

Fire out a load of guesses and see what hits! A shotgun statement is broad but doesn't *appear* like a meaningless generalization, i.e. not too specific but not too vague either. This is how TV psychics begin: "I'm being shown someone with a name beginning with M . . .?" It's the kind of thing that people might overlook as applicable to everyone in the room if they instantly connect with it themselves. One way this is done is to focus not on factual details, but on emotional content, which some people are very willing and ready to connect with.

This technique takes a little adaptation for everyday use. It needs to be possible to drop and move on from your statement if you are wrong in your guess. If you're right, you need to grab it and run with it.

"You seem like the type to really be into sports . . ."

"Uhh . . ."

"But not the usual sports, obviously. More things like gymnastics and dancing."

"Dancing? God no, I have two left feet. But I do a Zumba class once a week."

"I knew it! See? You can always tell when a person is very physically active . . ."

Technique 2: Barnum Statements

This technique is also called the Forer effect or, in psychological terms, the personal validation fallacy. We've already seen an example in the mini cold reading we did above. Human beings have an inbuilt capacity to take vague statements and connect them to their own personal lives, making private links and connections to what is objectively neutral information.

The hallmark of a Barnum statement is hedging or non-committal phrasing such as "sometimes" or "occasionally." This covers all bases and makes a claim without being too strong. If the other person doesn't connect to your prediction, it's not a problem—after all, you only said it happened sometimes, or *could* happen. Horoscopes work on this principle. If Leo's prediction for the day is "you may encounter some minor difficulties either in work or love," it's hard to imagine who *wouldn't* find the prediction come true!

A good Barnum statement is a win-win— either you're on the nose or you subtly fish for the other person to reveal information by how they respond to your "miss." Barnum statements are like verbal Rorschach blots—they are vague enough that other people can project their own meaning onto them.

"I'm very intuitive, you know, and I can tell that you're someone with strong personal opinions."
"Hm, pretty much."
"Sometimes you agree with people, but I think that occasionally, you have a few unconventional ideas about things."
"Ha, how did you know?"

Notice how the above exchange could have gone in a completely different direction:

"I'm very intuitive, you know, and I can tell that you're someone with strong personal opinions."

"Strong opinions? Really?" (Said doubtfully.)

"Oh, absolutely. Sometimes you agree with people, sure, but I think that occasionally, you have a few unconventional ideas about things."

"Yeah maybe. Most people think I'm pretty easy going. But I do stick up for myself when it's important."

"That's exactly what I mean. I can see that clearly."

The people in the above conversations could be polar opposites from one another, and yet respond to the same statement in very similar ways.

Technique 3: Ignoring the Misses

Closely connected to the above is the seamless, easy skipping over any time you actually make a guess that's wrong or make a claim that doesn't land. Cold reading is like fishing. Sometimes you have to send out a few lures to catch a fish—but if you catch nothing, you throw the lure out again, preferably without drawing too much attention to your failure!

As you engage in the conversation, you are homing in closer and closer, starting from generalizations and whittling down, using the person's responses to guide you. When you miss, you drop that approach. But when something sticks, you pursue that avenue and expand on it. Keep doing this and within a minute or two, it can genuinely seem like you have an eerily accurate understanding of the person you just met.

Minimize mistakes and amplify hits. You need to shift your strategy quickly and invisibly so that it almost appears as though you were on the right course from the very beginning. The typical psychic cold reading goes like this:

"I'm getting someone who's recently died? Maybe cancer or something to do with the heart?
(Crickets.)
"If not the heart, then I'm being shown something internal, in the body, like perhaps a gut or liver ailment. I'm seeing

someone who was a bit overweight? Someone who loved life and loved to eat?"

"My uncle, maybe . . .?"

(*Hit*. Psychic zooms in on this person.)

"Yes, it's a man, and I'm seeing that he really loved food, right?" (Knowing that this comment about eating prompted a response previously. The psychic ignores everything they said about cancer or heart and liver diseases.)

"Yes. He did love food . . ." (Who doesn't?)

"And was he a big man? Kind of a large guy?" (Vague statements that can be retroactively changed to mean *fat* or *tall,* depending on the response.)

"Well, not really. But he had a bit of a belly, I guess . . ."

"Yes, I see that . . . He was a middle-aged man? He was very troubled near the end, I think, in a lot of discomfort . . ." (If he's died, chances are he wasn't very young, and most men with bellies are middle aged. It's also a pretty good guess that he was uncomfortable before he died!)

"Yes! That's right! He had a lung infection." (Notice that the psychic has said nothing about lungs, but the person might not have noticed this mistake . . .)

Technique 4: Passing off Failures as Successes

Gradually, by ignoring the misses and emphasizing the hits, the fake psychic spins a tale that seems right on the money. But another related technique relies not on ignoring misses, but actually pretending they were hits all along. Again, your goal is to conceal the fact that you are actually guessing, and make it seem as though you had it right the very first time.

People who visit psychic shows are often quite willing to believe what they're told, and play along consciously or unconsciously. So, if the fake psychic has to massage the truth a little to alter the meaning of what they said *retroactively*, the audience might go along with it. Let's say the psychic closes their eyes and makes a show of hearing messages from beyond, then opens their eyes and claims they're being shown the name Elizabeth.

No takers from the crowd. "Ellie? Eliza? A name beginning with *El* . . . something like that?" the psychic continues. No dice. They try again.

"I'm seeing a woman's face, blue eyes, recently passed . . ."

"My aunt Linda passed recently."

"Ah, that's it! It wasn't Ellie, but the letter L, as in Linda."

"Ah, but she had brown eyes."

"Yes, I know. But she's showing me blue eyes for some reason . . . Did blue eyes have any significance for her . . .?"

And so on. At a push, a clever faux-psychic will stick to a story that nobody is buying and simply claim that the error is on the side of the living, or that someone is not sharing all the details they could. More than a few psychics have tried to pass off misses as a secret that the living simply don't know yet, or just claim that the clue will make sense in time.

Worst-case scenario, a miss can be covered up by blending it in with something that is true or couldn't help but be true. For example, "Okay, she's laughing now. She says don't worry about the blue eyes thing. She has a great sense of humor, your aunt, doesn't she? She's telling me to tell you not to worry about her, and that she's fine."

Technique 5: Keeping it Vague

It might seem pretty bold to claim to have supernatural abilities and perform in front of a crowd, but much of the success of fake TV psychics comes down to the fact that many of them are actually rather conservative in their "predictions." When you boil it down, what they say is not all that special . . . or precise.

Keeping vague keeps your options open and ensures that you make claims that have the highest probability of being correct or close to it. This then buys you time—and in that time, you can gather more information by observation. Under-promise and overdeliver—it's far better than overpromising and losing the confidence or faith of the person you're talking to.

Conversations are living, dynamic things. If you hope to extract information from people in ordinary life, you need to learn to dial up your observation skills while *gently* steering the conversation. You can't force the direction of the conversation too much because you need to be ready to perceive what's going on with your audience and adjust immediately. In time, you can firm up your statements.

For example, a psychic may make a vague claim just to see what the response will be. If it's vague enough, they can move on or shift the direction quickly.

"I see a brick house . . ."
"I'm feeling that he was in a lot of confusion and discomfort before he died."
"I'm sensing you had a strong connection with your mother."

Just as you would with Barnum statements, you want to make claims that are universal without seeming like they are (although a word of warning: don't make the mistake of using insensitive stereotypes about groups of people—that's unlikely to go down well!). Psychics are essentially in the business of telling people what they want to hear. Their audience might be so willing to hear it that they will round up almost any statement to fit the bill. So, a TV psychic could say, "I'm sensing that someone in the audience tonight has been doing a lot of soul searching lately," and two dozen people in the room will quietly believe that *they* are the ones being referred to.

It's a bit ironic that you can create this feeling of personal connection most effectively when you use general and vague statements, but hey, cold reading is not about appealing to human beings' rational side! Psychics have a great backup plan to cover up for any mistake—they are after all hearing transmissions from the "other side" and a few crackles in the transmission are to be expected, right? So, when a psychic is making a big deal about seeing things in a hazy light, or hears an indistinct voice, an unclear image, a hunch, a strange feeling they can't nail down—you know that they are either fishing for something firm to hold on to, or else covering up for a mistake recently made.

In everyday life, you can use vagueness in much the same way as a psychic uses it: to buy time. Make gentle Barnum-like statements but keep open ended, and wait until the other person gives you something to work with. If you are patient, you may be surprised how often people are willing to jump in and supply you with just the information you thought would be concealed.

A psychic can, as a last resort, claim that the spirit world sometimes speaks in riddles, or that you're tired today and not hearing as clearly. In everyday life, vagueness is a clever way to shunt the conversation back to the other person until you have something more definite to say. Make a loose, non-committal claim and then ask them a question or see how they respond. As a rule, it's always a good idea to start with general, vague statements and work from there, allowing the other person to guide you.

A closely connected technique is often called the "rainbow ruse," and its vagueness lies in the fact that you are essentially saying two opposite things at once, i.e. it's contradictory. There is some overlap here, again, with Barnum statements. The key to a rainbow ruse is to make a claim that sneakily covers *all* possibilities, so that the psychic is always going to be perceived as accurate no matter what.

"You are an introverted and shy person, but when you are with people you know and trust, you can have a wild and outgoing side that comes out."
"You are a very kind and considerate person, but there have been times when you have showed particular cruelty to people you were unhappy with."
"You are a person who knows what they want in life, but there have been times in the past that you have felt very unsure of what you're doing."

These sentences link two opposite ideas by varying things like mood (you're like X except when you're unhappy; then you're like Y), time (you're like X but at times can be like Y), and potential (you're like X but you have the capacity to be Y if you wanted).

It sounds too easy on the surface, but statements like this work because human beings are incredibly complex and often *do* possess two contradicting beliefs, traits, or desires. In addition, most people have a range of experiences that change over time, and, when hearing a rainbow ruse, will simply attach to the part of the statement that seems most relevant to them at that particular moment. It is the *response* to the claim that tells you so much, rather than the truth of the claim. In other words, it's almost irrelevant whether someone is or isn't an introvert, but if they choose to grab hold of that part of the claim and expand on it, you know that *they like to think of themselves* as introverted. And that brings us to our final technique.

Technique 6: Watching for Reactions

Our final technique is perhaps the most important, since the other five will be fairly useless unless combined with it. One half of cold reading is what you put out into the conversation, and the other half is what you are gathering back up again. You are not just making strategic guesses, but carefully watching how these guesses fall so you can run with them or drop them entirely. You are always, always looking for clues.

Have you noticed that psychics seldom offer their services over email or text? This is because most of them need face-to-face interaction. If they cannot tell how any one statement is being received by their audience, they can never really move things forward. Nothing will stop a cold reader dead in their tracks faster than someone who is expressionless and shows no response to what they're being told.

In TV psychic shows, people are happy to raise their hands or verbally say yes or no to claims. But even minor reactions can give you an idea of whether you're on the right track or not. If you're lucky, a person will happily give you information. For example, "No, that's not right. I think that maybe refers to my uncle? Or my cousin, maybe?" But if the other person is keeping it quiet, you can still watch their body language and facial expression to see if you're getting close.

As a rule, people noticeably respond to things that *do* apply to them. If the person is sitting stony-faced while you're talking, but suddenly shifts in their seats and seems to widen their eyes a little at the mention of the word "cancer," you can guess that cancer is somehow relevant to them. At psychic shows, after all, people are waiting anxiously to see whether something will be said about them—when it is, they can't help but light up, smile, or give other clues that they are suddenly paying attention.

The trick is that the person having these reactions isn't really aware that they're communicating this to anyone else. It looks on the surface like you are making guesses about them, but in reality, there is a dialogue going on between you both, only a subtle one.

Even more subtle is using general powers of observation to "read" people before they've even had a chance to react to what you're saying. The techniques we discussed in earlier chapters can be used to great effect here. Look for wedding rings, tan lines, baby food stains, expensive shoes, religious jewelry, tattoos. Notice if someone is slouching, leaning forward eagerly, frowning, crossing their arms, or looking exhausted. Sure, little things like this are not much in themselves, but they add up quickly if you're paying attention.

A great way to practice this skill is simply to observe people more often. Try a bit of "people watching" and observe others where they are not observing you and where verbal communication is off the cards—for example, in a busy street or airport. Look at people and guess who they are, their age, where they're from, what matters to them, what makes them sad, what their hopes and dreams are, what kind of car they drive, what work they do, what accent they have . . .

If you can just practice seeing what's in front of you (without stereotyping or entertaining prejudice), you'll soon be astonished by just how much people are already telling you about themselves long before they get into conversations with you. Ask—what stage of life is this person in, and what is statistically most likely for that age group? What socioeconomic group do they belong to, and what primarily concerns people in that group? What social and cultural markers do they have, and what does this tell you about who they are, or who they want to be? Practice often enough and it may even become second nature.

For instance, you might unconsciously register a person's clothing, demeanor, hairstyle, voice, and gestures and instantly recognize them as someone who is gay, or

Italian, or afraid of aging, or a nurse, or whatever. You may make a "guess" about them and surprise yourself by how accurate you are. True, people are all unique, and you may often be off the mark. But remember that in cold reading, you don't have to be right—just close enough.

Make a vague claim or a Barnum statement and watch what happens. Speak slowly to give the other person time to react to you.

As amusing as all this is, chances are you're not literally going to attempt to practice cold reading for real (although it's a fun practice so long as everyone is informed about what you're doing!). Cold reading understandably has a bad reputation, but there are intelligent ways to use these principles in ordinary conversation without being underhanded.

In reality, all these techniques blend into one. Keep things open, universal, and vague at first, and then fine tune the direction the conversation is going based on what the other person is giving you. Tailor your approach according to their response. Keep things light and flowing. You'll be surprised at how quickly you can get people to say, "Wow! How do you know so much about me?"

Takeaways

- We can improve our information extraction skills by following some of the techniques used by fake psychics when they do "cold reading."
- General principles for cold reading include being subtle, open-ended, and allowing the other person to guide you—without them realizing that you are not doing anything magical but merely working with the information that *they* provide.
- Shotgun statements are random statements made in order to see what response you get so you can follow it up on what sticks.
- Barnum statements are those that are likely to be perceived as relevant to individuals, even though they apply to almost everyone. Barnum statements are broad guesses that look specific but

168

actually have a high probability of being on the mark.

- When using shotgun or Barnum statements, a cold reader can also ignore their misses and focus on their hits, concealing the fact that they are guessing.
- Another way to mask misses is to pass them off as successes retroactively, or rework your claim to make it seem as though you were right all along.
- Cold readers deliberately keep things vague to start with, and then fine tune their approach according to the feedback they receive. They begin with a non-committal, low-stakes guess and then, by degree, inch closer to the truth using their audience's response or lack of it.
- A key principle in cold reading is to pay attention to reactions of all kinds, including nonverbal ones.
- Expert cold reading combines all of these techniques seamlessly and swiftly to give the impression that the "psychic" has plucked accurate information from the air, when in reality, it has been fed to him unwittingly by the audience all along!

Chapter 5. Interrogation (Sort of)

From the dazzling world of fake psychic cold reading (that's sarcasm), we now move on to the arguably more higher profile world of FBI agents, private detectives, and special investigators who are paid to dig out the truth no matter what. Just like with the fake psychics, however, we are not studying these proven interrogation techniques because we literally hope to one day be Jack Bauer in a dark room somewhere torturing the enemy. Rather, we can use some of the fascinating research and insights in this field to apply to our everyday lives.

If you become really good at extracting information from people using the following techniques, your "target" will not even bc aware that you have practiced any techniques at all. As with the tricks we've explored from faux psychics, the best interrogation techniques are not showy and pushy—instead, they're subtle, gentle, and invisible. When you are mining for information in this way, you get used to the fact that you will seldom get a straight answer from anyone. But, what *other* information can you get in the process? What else is their answer telling you, and what other guesses could you make with what you are given? Let's take a closer look.

Technique 1: Playing it Cool

Think about it: the whole reason you have to employ subtle techniques of info-extraction in the first place is because people, for whatever reason, are reluctant to share that information directly. If you give an impression of someone deliberately trying to force that information from the person, they will (correctly) perceive your questioning as a threat or intrusion and deliberately shut down.

On the other hand, if you can practice the fine art of informality, you can get the information you want without having the person raise their guard, or feel suspicious or put on the spot. The important thing is that it does not *feel* like an interrogation to them. If you are relaxed, casual, and non-threatening, you will almost always get a more revealing response than if you come across as someone who wants something.

You might even behave as if you were trying to ask a question or find information, but have now given it a rest and the "interrogation" is over. In an offhand way, as though to communicate that the information they share with you is only of minor importance anyway, ask your question on the way out, before the conversation officially begins, or in some other non-committal way.

As an example, consider a manager who has an interview with a potential recruit, shakes their hand at the end of the meeting, and then invites them to a quick coffee in the cafeteria. The interviewee, feeling that the interview is over, relaxes a little, lets their guard down, and answers questions far more easily. The manager can slip in a pertinent question or elicit information just as he's casually waving goodbye to the interviewee, who has no idea that the most important part of the meeting took place in those final few minutes.

Many people have gotten complete confessions out of those who felt that the interrogation was paused or over, or else believed they were no longer being seriously listened to. It sounds so simple, but it's remarkably effective: people put up defenses when they think they are being questioned, but drop them when they think they aren't. Solution: question people without them really knowing they're being questioned.

For example, a policeman tells a suspect they'll begin the questioning when his partner arrives. In the meantime, he takes out his phone to fiddle with it, curses his reception, and casually asks what network the suspect is on, seemingly not interested in the answer as he carries on fiddling with his phone. The suspect answers, feeling it's nothing more than casual chit chat, unaware that this is the only piece of information the officers are really after.

As another example, consider someone who says in a very relaxed manner, "Oh, okay, thanks for meeting me today. That's all I had to talk to you about. Can I call you a cab? You're heading east, right? Since you're at the Marriott?" The question about where someone was staying might have come across as incredibly intrusive if it had been asked straight out, but here seems natural and innocent.

"My friend was telling me this story the other day about a blind date he was on, It was hilarious. He's always complaining about being single—you're single right?— and I keep telling him he has awful taste in women . . ." This speech is delivered so casually, it seems like the question embedded in it is just an aside. It's also asked so quickly that the other person may automatically nod or shake their head or give some indication of an answer before even thinking about what they're being asked—far less stressful for both parties than asking more directly!

Technique 2: Pulling a Columbo

In the 1970s, a TV show detective called Columbo was so skilled at gently easing information out of people that his name became associated with the technique. Much like the previous technique, Columbo's skill lay in his successfully giving the impression of being non-threatening, casual, and maybe even a little stupid. The technique is pretty straightforward:

1. Get people talking freely and carelessly
2. Slip in a question when their guard is down
3. Show no indication of what's happened

For step one, gain rapport by engaging in open-ended, easy, casual conversation. Do your best to appear harmless and unimportant. You want to seem as though you are kind of at a loose end and not looking for the conversation to go one way or the other—i.e. you are not especially invested in their answers. This creates a sense of safety and informality. If you like, you could further disarm the other person by giving the impression that you are not just harmless, but a little bit incompetent. Look a bit lost or confused. Ask a few questions that genuinely do not cost the person anything to answer, to build up a sense of trust.

Then you can quietly slip in the question you really *do* want them to answer. You may not even ask a question at all. "Ask" indirectly by making a comment that the other person will then willingly (and seemingly of their own free will) volunteer information in response to. For example, say something you have a feeling they might vehemently disagree with—few people can resist correcting someone who's wrong or stepping in to defend a choice or preference.

Let's say you have a suspicion your unfaithful spouse met a lover at a restaurant, and you, in casual chat, mention off-hand that the place has been shut for months. Then you keep quiet and notice whether they jump in and say, "No, it's not. It's definitely open."

You could also appear to be talking about yourself—people are often more ready to share information about themselves when they feel they are simply agreeing with someone else. Maybe you want to find out who took your sandwich from the office fridge (not quite true detective work, sure, but important!). You casually mention the next day, "I had the most amazing ham and cheese sub yesterday!" If you do it casually enough, there's a strong chance they chime in with, "Me too!" especially if you prime the conversation by asking several questions beforehand that you know they will inevitably agree with. Success—you now know who the sandwich thief is.

The Columbo technique is also great for detecting someone who is lying to you. You could try repeating the same seemingly innocent question throughout the conversation, playing up being a little bit slow or forgetful, and watching carefully to see how the other person responds, maybe even setting the scene for them to make a mistake in their story or reveal a tiny clue you can follow up on. A doctor might be trying to get to the root of his patient's claim that he never touches alcohol, and then casually chat to him about the weekend and his own trip to the pub to get the patient to accidentally confess that . . . that's where they spent their weekend, too.

Here's the trick about both the Columbo technique and playing it cool, though: it doesn't really matter if you get the one hundred percent perfect answer to your question. *Any* little bit of information is worth something. The person might not reply at all—but that doesn't mean you cannot gather something from their body language or facial expression. Sometimes, a person's sudden and obvious refusal to answer a question when they were happy to answer all others tells you everything you need to know.

- Avoid confrontation—don't deliberately say, "I don't believe you," since nothing will get a person feeling more defensive, especially if they are lying or trying to hide something.
- Don't make a big show of listening. Yes, you are paying ultra-close attention, but don't broadcast this. Turn your body slightly away, act casual and relaxed, and even use a little humor to lower the perceived stakes of the interaction.
- Play dumb. Ask the other person to speak plainly and obviously, and

explain their story carefully. While they are assuming you're a bit dim, they may accidentally reveal more than they bargained for. "I forgot, where did you say you got your sandwich from?"

- If in doubt, ask people to repeat themselves. This puts stress on any story they may be telling you without it appearing that you are interrogating them. Watch for signs of stress or inconsistencies. What happens when you press on those inconsistencies? A person telling the truth usually doesn't care, but someone who is lying may grow flustered, defensive, or suddenly avoidant.

- Maintain plausible deniability. At no point must it be obvious that you are fishing for information.

Technique 3: False Replay

This is another technique that's great for catching out deception or lies. It works because liars have quite a difficult task to do—they need to construct and keep straight what could be quite a complex story. The more complex the story, however, the more chance there is of them muddling it up and revealing the lie. It takes a little extra cognitive power to hold two things in your mind—the truth and the lie. Remembering to tell the lie takes effort and time, but if you can trip up the liar quickly enough, they may make a mistake.

One way to do this is to make a mistake *for them*, and see how they react. For example, tell them the story they told you all over again, but this time make a mistake with one of the details you suspect to be a lie. Make it seem like you have genuinely messed this detail up. Now, watch very closely how they respond to this "mistake." If someone is telling you the truth, they may be at most a little annoyed and keep reiterating the same thing again.

If they're not, though, they may suddenly become anxious. This is because you've given them a slightly bigger cognitive load, i.e. asked them to keep track of a complex thing—a mistake about a lie that they know is false but must pretend is true. When someone is trying to stay ahead of their story, they may appear distracted, stiff, agitated, angry, and suddenly close or tighten their body language. They may try to stop you from recounting the story or wave it all off by saying they can't remember anyway or it doesn't matter.

One particularly useful response is if the person happily goes along with your mistake without attempting to correct you. Think about it: they think that *you* believe this new version and have forgotten what you told them earlier, so they may see no point in reiterating the "truth." Listen carefully to a person who retells their own story—truth-tellers tend to stick to the same story no matter what, telling it over and over again, whereas liars tend to overembellish, adding too much detail and seemingly adding more with every retelling in the belief that these details will make the lie seem more realistic.

If you suspect that a particular detail is a lie, repeat the story back to them, paraphrasing the details, and then casually slip in what you think the truth is as a "mistake." A particularly effective faux-mistake to make is one that shines the other person in a good light—who would want to correct something flattering? If you do it quickly, or repeat it a few times here and there in different words, you may be surprised to find the other person slips up and agrees, or fails to correct you. Their brain registers this "mistake" as the truth (because it is), and in a confusing moment, they may default to the cognitively simpler explanation—i.e. the truth.

Even if the false replay technique doesn't confuse the person trying to lie, it may well fluster them. Most liars spend a little while rehearsing the fib beforehand so they can recite it as naturally as possible. But if you force them to tell their story in a different order, pick it apart, ask them unexpected questions about it, make mistakes yourself, play at being confused, and so on, this carefully rehearsed lie flies out the window and they need to think of something on their feet. This is where you are watching carefully to observe any signs of stress, distraction, agitation, or panic—sure signs they're doing a little extra cognitive processing (i.e. telling a big fat lie!).

Technique 4: Leading Questions

So far, we have been using questions in two ways: first as a way to deliberately extract information from someone, and second to pose a topic or idea and then watch and interpret their reaction, regardless of their verbal response. But questions can be used in another way. Leading questions do exactly that—they *lead* the listener to certain thoughts and ideas and away from others. This technique might be especially useful if you already know or have a good idea of the "right" answer, i.e. you suspect a lie or want a confession.

A leading question actively persuades thought in a particular direction, but also subtly shuts off other avenues, directing the conversation in one way and not in another. By now, you can probably guess that what makes a leading question is not just the words you use, but your tone of voice, body language, and so on. Use your tone, posture, and voice volume to "nudge" the other person in the direction you want them to go.

There's a reason that questioning of this kind is frowned upon in formal police interrogations, and for good reason: it's an advanced technique that is not appropriate in all situations, and could even do more harm than good. If you are comfortable and skilled with other techniques discussed in this book, you can begin using leading questions, but simply be aware that doing so incorrectly may make your life more complicated!

One way to lead someone is to ask a question that rests on a particular assumption; in answering the question, they confirm the assumption. If you wanted to determine the truth of the rumor that your workplace was firing a third of the staff soon, you could casually ask, "So how many people are getting laid off next quarter?" By doing so, you're behaving as though the fact that there *are* people getting laid off is already a given. You might get lucky and have them say something like, "How do you know people are getting laid off?"

This technique works because you are not asking an open-ended question like, "Are people getting laid off?" The question itself is framed as a yes/no choice, so the person will obviously take a moment to think about it. And then lie and say no.

Another way to use questions to lead is to carefully choose *when* you will ask them, i.e. after a particular context is set, or you've "primed" the listener in some other way. You could share your opinion, for example, or make an emotional appeal, then ask your question:

"Oh, it's very common to lie on a tax return, we see it happen all the time. Have you ever done something like that?"
"Ah, well, personally I can't stand the woman. Was it you who left her that rude comment?"

A common but effective technique is to get the other person to answer affirmatively to a whole string of questions first, eventually leading to a question you also want them to say yes to. This is a salesman's tactic, but it can also be used to work around people's defenses and create a kind of conversational momentum.

"So you were at Dave's house on Tuesday?"
"Yup."

"And that means you couldn't possibly have been anywhere else."

"Yup."

"You were there till 9 p.m., and by that time, my bicycle had already been broken. Somehow."

"Yup."

"And Dave said you were with him that day because you asked him to say that."

"Yup. I mean, uh . . ." (Sudden red face.)

Try adding some conversational sticks and carrots in the mix to gently nudge a particular response:

"This bill would cause major environmental havoc, obviously. So what are your feelings about it?"

"Would you rather live in Anchorage or sweet, sunny California?"

Note here, however, that unlike a salesman or marketer, you are not trying to manipulate someone to say what you want them to say, but to say the *truth*, which they may be withholding for whatever reason. So, if you suspect they hate the new bill or secretly want to move to California but haven't told anyone, the above questions could help you tease out that information.

In general, closed questions are invariably more leading than open ones. The fewer possible logical responses the person can give, the more you can herd them toward the answer you're looking for. Make it easier and simpler for the other person to say "yes" if that's what you're looking for. So, use phrasing like, "Is it true that . . .?" or, "Do you agree that . . .?" Psychologically, questions framed this way almost seem to beg for agreement or an affirmative response.

You could add a "questions tag" at the end for extra impact:

"There's something you're not telling me, isn't there?"
"We can rely on your support, can't we?"
"Everyone agrees about this, don't they?"

Questions tags usually take this form, with a negated, abbreviated verb followed by a pronoun, for example:

". . . wouldn't we?"

"... didn't they?"
"... haven't you?"

Sometimes a question tag can be phrased in the positive to negate the previous sentence (for example, "You wouldn't do that, would you?"), but for our purposes, this is less effective as, psychologically, it may be perceived as more open-ended than we'd like.

Question tags are powerful things. They essentially take a statement and merely pose it as a question. But it's not really a question, is it? (You see what I did there, right?) It's something that's presented as so obvious that nobody would seriously question it. In other words, the person asking this question is not *expecting* you to disagree or even giving you the option to—and that can be a surprisingly strong motivator to agree.

As you can probably tell, changing the way you frame questions is a fascinating and complex skill to master, but be cautious. Information obtained under torture is useless. You don't want to bully, coerce, or threaten people. You don't want them to just say whatever they think you want to hear. Saying something like, "Come on, say you'll do it. You wouldn't say no to me, would you?" is likely to twist someone's arm and make them do what you want. But if you want to extract genuine information from people, you may need to be a little subtler.

Technique 5: Be Provocative

This one is a little easier.

"So, how did you do so well on that assignment? Did you just cheat and copy it all?"
"Where were you the other night? Out blowing all your money at a strip club, I guess."
"Why did you really come visit me, hm? Come to tell me some nasty gossip?"

You ask a question and then immediately follow it up with quite an outrageous statement. Be a little rude, bordering on insulting if you like. This is a potent tool that needs to be used sparingly. Send off a little firecracker and watch very, very carefully what response you get.

Shocked laughter or surprise is to be expected from people who don't have much to hide. At worst, they'll be puzzled and your "joke" will fall a little flat. No problem—you're not trying to practice your stand up, but get closer to the truth. If, on the other hand, the person suddenly goes pale, responds with utter panic and fear, or immediately becomes disproportionately enraged, you can assume that you've hit a nerve and that your provocative statement is closer to fact than fiction.

The only disadvantage of such a technique is that you may "show your hand" and put the other person on the defensive, so it's best to use this approach when you've already tried everything else. The thing about lying, being evasive, avoidant, and so on is that it can hide easily in all the expected conventions of civilized conversation. Many deceptive or evasive people succeed precisely because they know that even if people have their doubts, few are cheeky enough to come out and say something directly.

If you do, though, you create a momentary suspension of the conversational rules. And those few split seconds when the person is trying to react to your curve ball may be all you need to catch a glimpse of what they *really* think and feel. This technique is a little underhanded since you are deliberately creating a state of high emotion, intimidation, shame, or annoyance in the other person. But if you can do this, and unexpectedly, they may be on the back foot for just long enough for you to see through any lies.

Once you've fired off this provocative shot, you can reel it in again by acting as though it was just a joke, or playing coy or innocent, as though you simply had no idea that this would cause such a reaction in them. Don't worry about the provocative statement being true. That's not the point. The point is to spur an emotional reaction that then points you to the truth one way or another.

A calm, direct response is likely not concealing anything, as is a simple reiteration of the facts. Likewise, a person who comfortably responds as though the statement is a joke is probably not being evasive or dishonest. But "protesting too much" or getting emotional is a big clue you've hit a little too close to home. Compare:

"Where were you the other night? Out blowing all your money at a strip club, I guess."
Answer 1: "What? Don't be silly. I was at work."
Answer 2: "Haha, you got me, now my secret's out. The place should give me a loyalty card at this point."
Answer 3: "What! No! How could you even say that! That wasn't a strip club; it was a *gentleman's lounge!*"

Finally, one clever way to use provocative statements is to in effect give people permission to make a much milder, more moderate statement—the one you want them to really confess to. So, let's say you're a doctor who wants a diabetic to admit that they've been cheating on their specially prescribed diet.

"Why are your sugar levels this high? I bet you've eaten nothing but M&Ms for a month."

"No way, I've been following the diet."

"Really? Maybe you just ate a whole cake before you got here."

"No . . ."

"*Half* a cake?"

"Well, I had a few cookies, that was all. Just a few . . ."

Obviously, hyperbole like this may or may not work, and it depends on your relationship with the person and what's appropriate. Naturally, some people will always respond emotionally to hyperbole or provocative statements, whether they are true or not, so keep this in mind and be careful.

Technique 6: Gauge Response, Not Answers

As we've seen, the kinds of questions we are learning to ask are questions whose literal *answers* we're not strictly interested in. Rather, it's the person's overall *response* to the question itself that we are gauging, regardless of what they verbally answer to the question. The question can almost be thought of as a diversion or distraction—what we are really hoping for is to trigger an automatic and unguarded emotional or nonverbal reaction.

Have you ever noticed how people basically never listen to what politicians say? The politician is lying, people know he is lying, and the game seems to be about figuring out the truth *beyond* the perfectly written but totally insincere public speech. This is a very cynical extreme, but it can point us to a useful axiom in the world of extracting information from others: that the information we want is often "between the lines."

Ask a question. Even if you receive a lie or a non-answer in return, the person cannot help but simultaneously have a nonverbal reaction to your question. Analyze *that*. Do they seem alarmed, confused, hesitant, certain, happy, miserable, guarded, open? How does their response to an important question compare to their response to a trivial one?
Does their reaction seem proportionate? Inappropriate? Unexpected?

To gauge people's emotional and nonverbal reactions, sneak in a few questions that look as though they're there merely to test their understanding or agreement. So, for example, you can ask, "How do you feel about this?" or, "Have I understood that correctly?" or, "Does that make sense to you?" Here, tag questions can also be used to encourage a response and keep up the flow and momentum of the conversation.

Of course, you already know the answer to these questions, but in asking them, you are encouraging the other person to respond to you. The more questions, the greater the response. While the other person will feel as though they are merely supplying you with verbal confirmation that they understand, etc., you are actually listening closely for another kind of information. The person being questioned may leave the conversation thinking that they have revealed nothing, but you will leave it having gathered a huge amount of nonverbal data.

These techniques and approaches are better understood with examples. Like the cold reading strategies we discussed in the previous chapter, our "interrogation lite" techniques have considerable overlap and are best used in combination. Consider the following conversation that includes a little of everything. It's a job interview where the interviewer suspects the candidate is not being entirely truthful, or at best is concealing a few key details that are important to know.

Interviewer: Can I get you some coffee? Two sugars? We've just had a new machine put in. It's great. It does this cool thing with the foam. (*Blah blah blah about coffee*— keeping things informal and unofficial to put the candidate at ease.)

Candidate: Oh, wow, yeah, this is good coffee!

I: Right? I think if a company can't provide good coffee, there's something seriously wrong with them.

C: Exactly! (Laughs.)

I: What was the coffee like at your old place? From your CV, it seems like you left under tense circumstances, didn't you?

(Still said pretty casually, with a tag question thrown in to make it easier to agree.)

C: (Slightly uneasy.) Uh, well, huh. The company was doing a lot of restructuring. The role I was originally onboarded for changed a lot over the five years I was there . . ."

I: You didn't like those changes? (This is quite provocative, especially as it's an interruption. Here, the interviewer watches for the response, not the answer.)

C: (Laughs nervously.) Well, when you put it that way, I guess not! I respect what they're doing with that department, but it wasn't a good fit for me anymore.

I: So you left?

C: I did. (The interviewer notices how quick and easy this answer is compared to some of the others.)

I: So is it that you were angry about the restructuring or that you feel that you couldn't keep up? (Again, quite provocative, and a closed, leading question.)

C: (Pausing to think.) Oh, it was neither. I just saw them going in a very different direction.

I: Okay, makes sense. So you were there for seven years (Pauses to see if the candidate will correct this flattering "mistake" . . . he doesn't.) but you called it a day when they started to change things up . . .

C: Yeah, we were just not on the same page. (Note how this answer is *not* a simple "yes" like the previous one, and more of the same scripted story.)

I: I mean, you look like the ideal employee on paper. They'd be crazy to let someone like you go. Come on, what did you do, steal the boss's favorite mug or something? (One final provocative statement.)

C: (Suddenly looking horrified.) God no. No. No I didn't do *that*. (Awkward silence, with lots of uncomfortable body language.)

The interviewer can't help but notice this sudden shift. After twenty more minutes, the interviewer returns to this topic a few more times and notices that not only does the story of his leaving change subtly with each retelling, but that the candidate is increasingly agitated, distracted, and even angry. They conclude the interview and later, after some digging, find out that the candidate was in fact fired after suspicions of embezzlement and fraud.

Takeaways

- To take our information extraction to the next level, we can use lighter, more relaxed versions of the interrogation techniques practiced by law enforcement.
- One key approach is to lower the person's defenses by not appearing to them as a threat. This can be done by being casual and informal, or even prying when official interrogations are over. The trick is to behave as though you're not especially invested in their answer.

- The Columbo technique relies on this impression of casualness so that a question can be sneakily slipped in and answered while the person's guard is down. Play dumb, ask people to repeat themselves, and maintain a degree of plausible deniability. Hide questions in comments or statements that the other person can't help but respond to—and reveal themselves.
- The false replay technique aims to confuse and disorient a liar and get them to slip up or confess. You repeat back their story but make a "mistake" with a crucial detail, and watch their reaction. A liar is most likely to ignore it, while a truth teller will correct you. Liars are also most likely to grow agitated, angry, or distracted with being asked to retell their story in different ways, or being asked about it repeatedly.
- Leading questions are typically closed questions that guide a person's response to where you suspect the truth lies. A question can be made with a built-in assumption, or you could lead a person with priming statements or question tags.

- Being provocative is a great way to de-stabilize someone and observe their reaction—disproportionate anger, fear, or distraction indicate you've hit a nerve.
- The golden rule is to gauge a person's complete *response* to a question, and not just their verbal *answer*. Use questions to trigger an emotional reaction and analyze this in context.

Summary Guide

- It's possible to extract loads of useful information from people merely by using the power of observation.
- First, observe the face, tiny, quick and involuntary movements of the face can "leak" a person's true emotions – there are six universal ones: anger, fear, surprise, disgust, happiness. Look for microexpressions that contradict what is said verbally.
- Ex-FBI agent Joe Navarro has some tips for reading body language, and they come from an understanding that body language is inbuilt, automatic and ancient, and based on fight, flight or freeze response in humans. For examples, "pacifying behaviors" like
- covering the neck can indicate the person is trying to manage stress.
- Note how the body is occupying space, and whether it is generally closed or open. Posture and gesture can tell you

about whether a person is assertive, aggressive, uncertain or fearful. Bodies expand when they are comfortable, happy, or dominant. They contract when unhappy, fearful, or threatened.

- Body language signals cannot be interpreted in isolation. Rather, first seek a baseline of behavior to help interpret a particular new observation – a baseline helps you identify incongruent behavior and spot a deception.
- Look for mirroring, pay attention to overall energy, and remember that body language is dynamic, so you need to gather as much data as possible. Then consider this data in context of history and the current environment.
- The voice is a part of the human body and speed, timbre, volume, pitch, and degree of control can signify emotional state. The body is a whole, with verbal and nonverbal mingling together.
- Reading "message clusters" helps us organize isolated observations, and note whether they are aggressive, romantic, assertive, deceptive ad so on, in aggregate.

- Asking questions is an active way to deliberately elicit information from a person, but they need to be targeted and not too obvious. A few seemingly casual hypothetical questions can reveal a person's deeper values, perspectives and goals, for example asking what their favorite movie is, what they would save from a fire, or what animal they see themselves as.
- Analyze the answers to these questions cautiously, and remember to place everything in context. Note *how* they answer, not just the content, and also not what isn't said. Use extrapolation to draw conclusions about what their answers say about them in a more general sense.
- Questions needs to be iterative and responsive to the context and the answers you've already received. Also think about behavior online and in emails, or "read" a person's possessions or home the way you would their body

205

language. Use these observations to guide your questions.

- Elicitation is more deliberate still, and uses a string of guiding questions to lead a person to give you precisely the information you're looking for, without it seeming that you are.
- Developed originally by the FBI, these techniques are really just ways to carefully work around conversational and societal norms to your advantage. They are effective because they work with human being's natural social and behavioral tendencies.
- For example, one tendency is towards recognition, or social connection. Use compliments or accurate observations to foster a rapport with someone or strengthen your connection.
- You can also elicit information by encouraging people to complain, and in doing so, reveal something previously hidden, or else tap into the human need to correct someone's error. Sued skillfully, most people cannot resist joining in on a complaining session or correcting an "error" you make.

- Playing dumb or using naivete or ignorance will also encourage some people to try to educate you, and share vital information, especially since you will seem so non-threatening.
- Finally, one technique is to say something quite dramatic to "shift the window" and then act as though nothing has happened; subtly, you may well elicit a revealing response. Silence can also be used effectively, since it encourages people to fill the gap with the information you want to know.

CHAPTER 3. COMFORT

- Trust has been shown to work in a linear fashion. The more you see someone, the more you trust them, regardless of interaction or depth. This is known as the propinquity effect, and can be used to your advantage in making people feel psychologically comfortable with sharing more with you.

- Credibility is a notch above trust; trust is about people feeling that they can believe you, and credibility is where people also feel that they can rely on you. There are also proven ways to create an aura of credibility around yourself. These include highlighting qualifications, showing your caring and empathy, showing similarity, being assertive, showing social proof, not contradicting yourself, and avoiding being overly polite.
- Eye contact is essential for building trust. If you aren't able to use eye contact, people will find you untrustworthy. The optimal eye contact period is around three seconds of eye contact at a time, with sufficient rest between gazes.
- Active listening is a valuable skill set that any person should master, but the techniques of active listening can also help you improve your elicitation abilities and gather more information about people. You need to comprehend, retain and respond to the information people are sharing with you.

- You can build rapport and connection in many ways, for example by restating, reflecting, summarizing, labeling emotions, probing (gently!) and using silence to encourage the other person to open up. Open-ended or leading questions (like those covered in the previous chapter) can subtly guide a person to open up to you.
- Avoid giving advice, lecturing, sermonizing or judging.
- Active listening techniques are best used when you would like someone to open up with you and share their true feelings. Other techniques are more appropriate for detecting deception.

CHAPTER 4. READ AND TELL

- We can improve our information extraction skills by following some of the techniques used by fake psychics when they do "cold reading."
- General principles for cold reading include being subtle, open-ended, and allowing the other person to guide you—without them realizing that you

are not doing anything magical but merely working with the information that *they* provide.

- Shotgun statements are random statements made in order to see what response you get so you can follow it up on what sticks.
- Barnum statements are those that are likely to be perceived as relevant to individuals, even though they apply to almost everyone. Barnum statements are broad guesses that look specific but actually have a high probability of being on the mark.
- When using shotgun or Barnum statements, a cold reader can also ignore their misses and focus on their hits, concealing the fact that they are guessing.
- Another way to mask misses is to pass them off as successes retroactively, or rework your claim to make it seem as though you were right all along.
- Cold readers deliberately keep things vague to start with, and then fine tune their approach according to the feedback they receive. They begin with a non-committal, low-stakes guess and then, by degree, inch closer to the truth

using their audience's response or lack of it.
- A key principle in cold reading is to pay attention to reactions of all kinds, including nonverbal ones.
- Expert cold reading combines all of these techniques seamlessly and swiftly to give the impression that the "psychic" has plucked accurate information from the air, when in reality, it has been fed to him unwittingly by the audience all along!

CHAPTER 5. INTERROGATION (SORT OF)

- To take our information extraction to the next level, we can use lighter, more relaxed versions of the interrogation techniques practiced by law enforcement.
- One key approach is to lower the person's defenses by not appearing to them as a threat. This can be done by being casual and informal, or even prying when official interrogations are over. The trick is to behave as though you're not especially invested in their answer.

211

- The Columbo technique relies on this impression of casualness so that a question can be sneakily slipped in and answered while the person's guard is down. Play dumb, ask people to repeat themselves, and maintain a degree of plausible deniability. Hide questions in comments or statements that the other person can't help but respond to—and reveal themselves.

- The false replay technique aims to confuse and disorient a liar and get them to slip up or confess. You repeat back their story but make a "mistake" with a crucial detail, and watch their reaction. A liar is most likely to ignore it, while a truth teller will correct you. Liars are also most likely to grow agitated, angry, or distracted with being asked to retell their story in different ways, or being asked about it repeatedly.

- Leading questions are typically closed questions that guide a person's response to where you suspect the truth lies. A question can be made with a built-in assumption, or you could lead a person with priming statements or question tags.

- Being provocative is a great way to destabilize someone and observe their reaction—disproportionate anger, fear, or distraction indicate you've hit a nerve.
- The golden rule is to gauge a person's complete *response* to a question, and not just their verbal *answer*. Use questions to trigger an emotional reaction and analyze this in context.